help

I'm a Frustrated Youth Worker!
A Practical Guide to Avoiding Burnout in Your Ministry

ZONDERVAN®

ZONDERVAN.com/
AUTHORTRACKER
follow your favorite authors

youth
specialties

**youth
specialties**

Help! I'm a Frustrated Youth Worker!: A Practical Guide to Avoiding Burnout in Your Ministry
Copyright 2009 by Steven L. Case

Youth Specialties resources, 300 S. Pierce St., El Cajon, CA 92020 are published by
Zondervan, 5300 Patterson Ave. SE, Grand Rapids, MI 49530.

ISBN 978-0-310-27888-7

Cover design by Toolbox Studios and David Conn
Interior design by Brandi Etheredge Design and David Conn

Printed in the United States of America

09 10 11 12 13 14 • 20 19 18 17 16 15 14 13 12 11 10 9 8 7 6 5 4 3 2 1

This book is dedicated to the memory of Lewis Collins.

Special thanks to:

Jay Howver, Roni Meek, Randy Southern, and the rest
of the staff at Youth Specialties.

Kent Crocket for his amazing (and lifesaving) book,
The 911 Handbook, which helped inspire this one.

The youth group and congregation of the Windermere
Union Church, United Church of Christ; Rev. Barton Buchanan;
Rev. Karen Curtis-Weakly; Rev. Richard McCandless; Rev. Mary
Haberkorn; Rev. Jim BeBee; Rev. Warren Langer; Rev. Bob Ma-
chovec; Rev. Jon Francher; Rev. Robert Dietrich; Rev. Bob Kuntz;
Rev. Libby Merkel; Deloris Dickinson; and all the others who
have taught me a lesson or two about working in a church.

Extra special thanks to Aprille and Eric and to my wife,
Becky, for her love and patience.

Contents

1. There's Always Somebody Willing to Pee in Your Froot Loops

Looking Out for Number One

It's Youth Sunday at River Run by the Ocean Forest Community Church, and—surprise, surprise—it also happens to be the senior pastor's vacation day. The church is reasonably filled because people want to hear what the youth group did on its mission trip. Frankly, most people probably just want to know what the youth group did with the money they donated for the trip.

Youth pastor Kevin is ready for his group's moment in the spotlight. He's lined up some of his best speakers to talk about the trip that involved riding 11 hours in a 15-passenger van and sleeping on the floor of a church in a distant city. Sort of a what-I-did-over-my-summer-mission-trip report.

First up, he's got Marc, who's always good for a laugh. Marc will lead off with his story about the lady in the shelter who had no teeth but kissed him anyway when he found her lost coat.

Next, Kevin's scheduled Jeanie, who will cry at the drop of a hat. Jeannie will talk about the little kids in the basement playroom and how they painted the walls to look like the Candy Land board game. Jeanie will start to cry about halfway through her presentation, and members of the congregation will likely follow suit.

After that, two other girls will present together and give a nice, just-the-facts-ma'am report of exactly what they did. Kevin's wild card this year is Alan, who has yet to tell anyone what he's going to talk about. "Trust me," he said. So that's what Kevin's doing.

Thirty minutes later, most of the congregation is in tears. As expected, Jeanie started the waterworks. Alan's talk, however, sent the audience over the edge. Alan explained how he went into the mission trip griping that his parents wouldn't buy him the new Nintendo game he wanted. He talked about striking up a conversation with a 17-year-old girl named Janice and then meeting Rachel, Janice's two-year-old daughter. Alan learned that Janice had been kicked out of her house when her parents found out she was pregnant. Rachel's father denied that the baby was his and cut off contact with Janice. Janice was forced to live on the street and in shelters for three months, until she finally found a place that would let her stay until her baby was born. From there, she moved in with a friend and stayed for a year, until her friend's live-in boyfriend started beating her and Rachel.

Alan managed to keep his composure until he got to the part about little Rachel getting smacked around. That's when he started to lose it. And that's when the congregation followed his example.

Alan talked about how, during the evening devotions, he questioned why God would let such a terrible thing happen. Then he heard Pastor Kevin talk about how God puts us on this planet to *be* the change—the answer to somebody else's prayers.

Alan wrapped up his talk by announcing that since coming back home, he's given away his entire video game system to a local shelter and has been volunteering there once a week. As a final touch, he invited the rest of the church to join him at the shelter next Wednesday.

After Alan came the slide-show presentation, which had been lovingly prepared by one of the students. With Ginny Owens singing "If You Want Me To" on the soundtrack, picture after picture flashed on the screen, each one showing youth group members in action. The congregation watched scenes of the kids they've known all their lives—*their* children—all grown up and sweating as they move furniture for an elderly woman. Next came a close-up of a drop of paint on the end of a ninth-grade girl's nose as she helps a child paint a large yellow bird on a wall. That was followed by a shot of Alan reading a story to little Rachel. By this time, any remaining dry eyes in the house have been moistened.

At the end of the song, Alan, in an impromptu gesture, stood up again and told the congregation how wonderful Kevin is and how everyone in the youth group really, really appreciates all Kevin went through and all he put up with. Then the youth group led the congregation in a standing ovation for Youth Pastor Kevin.

Then comes coffee hour.

Everyone is mingling and sipping coffee from Styrofoam cups and talking about what a wonderful job the youth group has done and how wonderful it is that they have someone like Kevin to lead their kids. And there Kevin stands, proud of his students to the point of tearing up himself, but at the same time basking in the glow of it all and mentally preparing his report for his next job review.

Emerging from the crowd to interrupt Kevin's reverie is Mr. Kettering, a staple in the church. He's almost 70, but he looks 50. He was the first one there with his chainsaw when the tree fell on the playground back in '85. He's the one who's there to shovel snow and change light bulbs and get one more year out of the furnace. He's the one who will stand up during congregational meetings to talk about how disappointed he is that such a major portion of the budget has to go to trivial things.

Mr. Kettering approaches Kevin and extends his hand. Kevin takes it. Mr. Kettering says, "That's all well and good, but I just wonder why we can't seem to serve the needy in our own community. I just think we're missing something when there are shelters right here that could use a good crew to work on them, too." He pats Pastor Kevin on the back and heads for the cookie table.

Suddenly everyone within earshot of the conversation starts wondering the same thing as Mr. Kettering.

The Inescapable Fact of Youth Ministry
No matter who you are...

No matter where you go...

No matter what you do...

You will *always, always, always* encounter somebody who's willing to pee in your Froot Loops.

Stop right here. Go back and read the preceding passage again. Then read it a third time. Keep reading it until you accept it as gospel truth; then we can move on.

You'll notice that Mr. Kettering didn't say, "You did a bad job" or "You shouldn't have gone on the trip." He simply peed in Kevin's Froot Loops.

Is that a gross analogy? Yes. Does it paint a vivid picture of the effect some people can have on others? You'd better believe it.

Sometimes perfectly well-meaning people feel it's their obligation to make sure you don't think you're quite as special as you think you are. These are people who can look at a beautiful tree, alive with the fiery colors of autumn, and see only a black trunk that could kill you if you ran into it hard enough. Whatever the situation, they can find a way to make it seem just a little worse.

There are strategies for dealing with such people and the criticism they bring, and we'll explore them later in the book. Before we get to that, though, here are five principles you need to remember:

1. People who pee in your Froot Loops can't see the ministry for the trees.
For a biblical example of Froot-Loop peeing, take a look at John 9:1-41. Here's how the situation might have played out.

Blind Man: Help me?

Disciples: Hey, Jesus, is this guy blind because of something he did, or something his parents did?

Blind Man: Help me?

Jesus: Why do you always need someone to blame for things? Watch this. (Jesus spits in the dirt, makes some mud, covers the blind man's eyes, and speaks to the blind man.) Now go wash off the mud.

Blind Man: Hey! I can see!

Bystander #1: Isn't he the one who was blind?

Bystander #2: Nah, that's just someone who looks like him.

(Previously) Blind Man: It's me! I can see! Jesus healed me!

Bystander #1: Who is Jesus? Point him out to us.

(Previously) Blind Man: Like I would know what he looks like? I was blind, for crying out loud.

Pharisee: How did you get your sight back?

(Previously) Blind Man: Jesus healed me.

Pharisee: Well, that settles it. Jesus is no Messiah. The Messiah wouldn't work on the Sabbath.

(Previously, Until Very Recently) Blind Man: Hellooooooooo? I can seeeeeeeeee.

Pharisees: (To the man's parents) Is this your son? Wasn't he born blind? How did this happen?

(Previously) Blind Man's Folks: Why don't you ask him?

Not-Blind-Anymore Man: Hey, morons, my eyes are working here. It's a miracle.

Pharisee: Tell the truth. What REALLY happened?

Not-Blind-Anymore Man: I was blind. Now I can see. What more do you need to know?

Pharisee: Go through it one more time.

Blind-No-Longer Guy: Why? Do you want to follow him, too?

[AUTHOR'S NOTE: Never say that to a Pharisee.]

Pharisee: (After much cursing and anger) Throw him out in the street!

(Previously) Blind Guy: Hey, idiots, stop looking in the rule book. There's not going to be an entry for a mud-and-water blindness cure.

Many Pharisees: Throw him out! Throw him out! (They do.)

Not-Blind-Anymore Man: Unbelievable.

Jesus: Do you believe that what happened to you was a miracle?

(Previously) Blind Guy: Do you know who healed me?

Jesus: What, are you deaf now, too?

Blind-No-Longer Guy: It's YOU!

Jesus: I'm doing these miracles so that those who are figuratively blind can see, too.

Not-Blind-Anymore Man: What's *figuratively* mean?

Right in front of them, the Pharisees had a living, breathing miracle. Yet they couldn't get their heads out of their own … uh, rule books, long enough to see it. Even the blind guy's parents got all wishy-washy ("Yeah, well he *looks* like our kid, but our kid was blind. This one can see. Maybe you should ask him").

Jesus' disciples were so busy trying to assign blame for the man's blindness that they didn't see the miracle, either. They were asking algebra questions in English Lit class.

The people who pee in your Froot Loops often do so because they can't see the evidence of God's work right in front of them.

2. Understanding is the key.

Some people have no concept of what's involved in youth ministry. They think youth workers hang out with kids—and don't do much else beyond that. Before you respond to such people, you need to take their cluelessness into account.

You can't really hold it against them if they don't know what your job entails. Just like you can't yell at an eight-year-old boy who just baked the worst cake ever. The kid's never baked before. He doesn't know how the ingredients go together. Imagine screaming, "Get your tail back in that kitchen and bake another one! And don't you let me see your face again until you can come out with something sweet and tasty!" Would you say that? No. You'd cut the kid some slack because he's never done it before. Do the same with those who pee in your Froot Loops.

3. You'll find a Mr. Kettering no matter where you go.

At my first church there was a woman named Irene who found something wrong with just about everything involving youth ministry. She threw around words such as *messy, rude, lazy, disrespectful*—and she didn't like the teenagers much, either.

When I moved to another city, I looked forward to the fact that I'd no longer have to deal with Irene. It turned out she was waiting for me at my new church—except there her name was Naomi. She may have looked different and had a different name, but it was Irene. She'd followed me. In fact, she's been at every church I ever worked for.

When you're thinking of taking a new job, you wouldn't ask yourself, "Will there be air at my new church?" You might wonder about whether or not you have a youth room, an office and a desk, but you wouldn't wonder about air. That's a given. So is a Froot Loop pee-er.

4. Don't start to question yourself.

Youth ministers are a strange bunch of people. We can lead a really great Sunday night meeting—one in which kids actually have a good time *and* participate in the discussion—and then hear one kid say, "That kinda sucked," on his way out, and we go home thinking, "The whole meeting sucked! What the heck am I doing here? These kids hate me!"

Don't allow the Froot Loop pee-ers to distract you. When Peter stepped out of the boat on the Sea of Galilee, undoubtedly there was someone in the boat saying, "You're going to get your cloak wet" or "Well, someone's feeling pretty full of himself today."

Peter sank because he took his eyes off Jesus and started paying attention to the storm. He suddenly thought, "What the heck am I doing here?"

We get ourselves into trouble when we start to pay attention to the storm around us and not Jesus. We hear a rumor about pledges being down for next year, or we walk by a committee meting and hear our name mentioned, and we start to question who likes us and who doesn't. We learn that one of the church's "power families" has been having trouble getting one of their kids to go to youth group meetings because "It's soooooooo borrrrrrrrrrring," and we start to consider ways to overhaul the ministry.

5. Remember—God put you where you are.

God has never said "Oops." Not once. He doesn't make mistakes. If you're in your church, serving your students, it's because that's precisely where God wants you. Don't ever let anyone try to convince you otherwise.

God put you where you are for a reason. You may not discover that reason until long after you've left, but you are where you are right now because God decided that's the best place for you at this moment.

Sometimes it's only a moment before you have to move on. God may use Froot Loop pee-ers to give you a push, but don't let anyone tell you your presence isn't part of God's purpose.

There's a reason for the term "wet blanket." People who are wet blankets can put out your fire. You may be able to deal with one, but when you get wet blanket after wet blanket piled on top of you, you'll find it's hard to move. Doing even the basics of your job will seem like a struggle, never mind trying to start a fire within your students.

Learning to deal wisely with Froot Loop pee-ers will help keep your fire burning—and keep you doing God's work—long after the pee-ers have run out of...uh...ammunition.

Memorize This
Eventually the stream dries up.

2. Do You Know What Those @!*# Kids Have Done Now?

Dealing with Church Members' Complaints

Years ago I worked as a full-time youth minister at a fairly large church. The senior pastor was a nice guy who cared mostly that the ministry of the church was getting done and not so much about office hours and office attire.

One Monday morning I arrived at the church around 9:20. Monday was the senior pastor's and associate pastor's day off. The education director and I took Fridays off. So it was a fairly quiet building on Mondays. I made my way down the hall humming The Who's *Baba O'Riley* (sometimes known as *Teenage Wasteland*), with a cup of my favorite bagel-shop coffee in my hand (Bruegger's hazelnut). I turned the corner and there was Mrs. Steel. She had removed a chair from a Sunday school room and was sitting right outside my office. I couldn't have gotten my key in the door without going through her ear.

What I thought when I saw her consisted of two words, neither of which I'll mention here. What I said was, "Good morning, Millie. It's good to see you. How are you?"

But it *wasn't* a good morning anymore. It *wasn't* good to see her. And at that moment I knew *exactly* how she was: She was ticked.

She looked at her watch and frowned as I fished my keys out of my pocket. I said, "You look like you have something on your mind." (I'd been in youth ministry for more than 10 years by that time. I could pick up on her subtle hints.)

She said, "Do you know what those darn kids have done now?" Only she didn't say "darn."

I invited her in and offered her a chair. My office was in the youth room, so I thought about asking her to join me on one of the many old couches in the room. Sitting on most of them was like sitting on the floor, and I thought she might get uncomfortable and leave more quickly.

However, I placed a chair in front of my desk and took my seat behind it. That's me, Mr. Professional Youth Minister. I said, "What seems to be the problem?"

She said, "Those kids leave this building a mess every Sunday night, and the Ladies Quilting Committee [not the real name, but you get the general idea] has to clean up after them. And we're sick of doing that."

Okay, let's leave Millie sitting there for a moment while we look at five basic reasons people complain.

Why Complain?

Understanding why a person is complaining will go a long way toward helping you respond to that person in an effective way. Here are five possible reasons you should consider when you receive a complaint:

1. Some people are born complainers.

That sounds simple, doesn't it? But it's true. Right now I could ask you to name five people you know who are just good-hearted people. They love life. They have a cheerful attitude. They are just plain fun to be around. Can you think of five? If these people exist then the opposite is true also. Some people are just complainers in their souls.

2. Some people complain to protect the status quo.

Occasionally you might run into someone who's made the church her second home—and seems to have a vested interest in protecting its sanctity. Let's face it. We're all pretty picky about who we let into our homes. If people are guests in your house, you don't expect them to put their feet on the table or make rude bodily noises at the dinner table. (Okay, as a youth minister, most of your houseguests are probably teenagers. So maybe you do expect such things. But we're talking about other people's expectations.)

If you're dealing with a lifelong church member, there's a good chance that person sees you as a "guest" in the house (church). Some of the things you do will be seen as an affront to the well-established rules and traditions of the house. Most of what you do will be seen as disrespectful to a select few members.

3. Some people complain because they are uninformed.

If the most visual thing you do in your ministry is play volleyball or Sardines, then that will be the perception people have of your group. Many youth workers have gone to the administrative board to request a day off, only to be asked, "What for?"

Mike Yaconelli once told a story about a youth minister who was told that the beach retreat he planned for the senior high group would have to come out of his vacation time because, after all, he was just hanging out with kids on the beach.

People complain about our ministry because they don't see it as "ministry." Part of our job has to be to keep the congregation informed of what happens after the game of Shuffle Your Buns. Write articles for the church newsletter that are more than Youth Event Calendars. Create activities such as "The Writing on the Wall" that involve the church members.

The Writing on the Wall
Tape a large sheet of butcher paper (or several sheets from an easel pad) and a marker on a string to a wall near the sanctuary. Choose a "hot topic" from your local newspaper or a national issue to talk about with your students some Sunday evening. Ask them to write their thoughts and opinions regarding the topic on the sheet of paper. Invite the older members of the congregation to write their own opinions on the topic. Keep the sheet up for a few weeks. It's a visual way to let the youth group participate in the life of the church without having to be the clean-up crew at the Men's Bible Study Pancake Breakfast.

4. Some people complain because they feel bad about themselves.

Unlike the people in the first category, whose complaints are driven by a superiority complex, these complainers complain out of their own insecurities. Low self-esteem doesn't end when teens grow up. Many people take their feelings of inferiority right into adulthood with them. And, as they did when they were teenagers, they often put other people down in an effort to make themselves look better. One of the best ways to do that is by complaining.

In one of my first churches, I served as the director of education as well as the youth director. I wrote a Christmas pageant and almost immediately had a mother in my office who wanted her daughter to be Mary. This woman had grown up in the church and had participated in a dozen or more Christmas pageants. She'd always wanted to be Mary, but never got higher billing than "Angel #2." (Apparently there was a progression of some sort in the annual casting.) This woman was insistent. And when her daughter was chosen to be the main shepherd, the woman began spreading a rumor that I didn't like her daughter.

One of the best strategies for dealing with this type of complainer is to give the person a sense of authority. Make sure this person has a say in the matter. If nothing else, you might ask, "Would you like to sit here or here while we talk?" or "Which day best accommodates your schedule: Tuesday or Wednesday?" Make sure, too, that you acknowledge the person's experience and wisdom. "How long have you been a member? Really? You've seen a lot, haven't you?

Advent: A Fresh Perspective

Volunteer your students to help retool your church's Advent traditions. Many churches simply print off something from the denomination Web site and hand it to the Smithers family members, who glance at it for the first time on their way to church, then read it aloud in front of the congregation while little Jimmy nearly sets himself on fire lighting the wreath.

Surely your students can come up with a better idea. Recruit some of your creative writers to knock out some skits. Let the performers in your group act out the frustrations of the season and then bring in the comfort of Scripture.

What advice can you give me?" Look for ways to turn the person's sense of helplessness into a sense of help-FUL-ness.

Finally, here's the reason for complaining you probably don't want to read about.

5. Sometimes there really is a problem worth complaining about.

Did you know that *youth ministry* is actually an English translation of the Hebrew words for "messy noise"? Youth ministry, by its very nature, is disruptive and loud. It doesn't get in line, stay in line, or respect traditions. It's defiant. It's disrespectful. And it's messy. When someone complains about "what those darn kids have done now," it may actually be a case of what those darn kids have done now.

I have many personal examples, which I won't go into here. Suffice it to say that any idea that includes a Nerf gun, 200 six-inch ceramic Santa statues, and a roof probably falls into the not-so-good category. "Endangering the lives of our children" may have been an overstatement at the board meeting, but I can see the point.

When It's Your Turn to Respond

As I mentioned earlier, the complainer's motive will dictate the way you respond to him. Whatever the motive, though, here are four principles to keep in mind:

1. God sent the critic.

That's a hard truth to deal with, isn't it? If we truly believe that all things happen for a reason, then we have to stop and ask ourselves, "Why did God send this person to me? What am I supposed to learn? Is this person here for my sake, or is God using me for something this person might need?"

Here's a prayer for you to try: "God, I am your servant and I need your wisdom. Amen." It's a great little prayer to use before board meetings, job reviews, job interviews, counseling sessions, and budget-justification meetings.

2. Tag backs aren't allowed.

Here's a little piece of advice from your Uncle Steve. Ready? When someone says, "Those kids leave this church a mess every Sunday!" the best thing to say is *not* "Yeah? Well, that purse doesn't go with those shoes."

Wrong response. Trust me. REALLY wrong response.

Counterattacking is not the way to endear yourself to a church congregation, no matter how much ammunition you may have. Sure, the temptation to shout back at someone is always there. But if the person is uninformed, has low self-esteem, or is naturally negative, shouting won't help.

Ask yourself this: How would you react if the complainer were one of your students?

Here are some quick tips:

1. Never respond immediately to an email.
Many complainers use email as a means of instant gratification.

Give yourself 24 hours to process the message. (At the very least, give yourself an hour.) A fired-off response only gets a fired-off response, and then you've got yourself a situation like the end of that Looney Tunes cartoon where Bugs and Elmer Fudd keep escalating the weaponry.

2. Say, "Let me see if I'm hearing you right," then repeat the complaint back to the person.

Sometimes when a person hears a complaint coming back, she may be willing to tone it down. If not, at least you've got a clear picture of what you're dealing with.

3. Promise a response.

Assure the person that you'll look into the matter—and then *actually look into it*. Thank the person for bringing it to your attention.

3. Two magic words can work wonders.

I must attribute this suggestion properly because it's saved my bacon on many occasions. This tip came from the Reverend Bob Machovec, a Methodist minister in Ohio.

Bob offered two magic words—*however* and *therefore*—to employ at the next meeting of the administrative board or the youth council or the subcommittee on monitoring youth activities or wherever your biggest collection of complainers congregates. Announce a new rule for the meeting: No one is allowed to say, "We've never done it that way before" or "This is the way we've always done it"—unless they follow it with the word *however* or *therefore*, and then keep speaking.

At first, some folks may chuckle and think you're kidding. But start calling them on it, informally to begin with, and then cement it as a policy. Make sure everyone understands that "We've never..." and "We've always..." may not be used as stand-alone phrases in your meetings.

Two things will happen. One, you'll cut down on the complaints from those who just like to complain. And two, you might actually get some great ideas from others in the group.

4. Find the truth of the matter.
Keeping a cool head and a calm demeanor can help you get to the truth of a complaint and then find a solution.

Let's go back to Millie, who complained that the youth group left the whole building a mess every Sunday night.

I asked Millie what she meant by "the whole building." She said she'd found a problem in the kitchen.

I asked her how big the mess was. I asked her when it had happened. By asking the questions and giving her a chance to unload her frustrations, we finally arrived at the truth of the matter.

Two of my guys had been tossing a basketball back and forth in the kitchen. (Bad idea.) They knocked over a two-liter bottle of Mountain Dew. (Oops.) Instead of cleaning it up themselves, they simply picked up the bottle and left the puddle. (REALLY bad idea.) For Millie, it became a matter of "darn kids" making a "huge mess" throughout the "whole building."

I promised to pay more attention to the group's activities and make sure the basketball was thrown in the appropriate areas. I also told her I'd make sure that individuals cleaned up their own messes from now on.

Did that stop Millie from complaining ever again? Of course not. But the next time she made an appointment to see me and then came in with specifics, not exaggerations.

It's important to remember not to take criticism personally. People will complain no matter who sits in the youth minister's office. It's not about you.

Unlike "wet blankets," complainers can actually ignite a situation. Like a campfire left unattended, their flames can spread. If you spend all your time putting out fires, how long do you think you'll last before you're burned out?

Memorize This
Jesus Christ couldn't please everybody.
Why do you think you can?

3. Oh, Yeah? Well, Same to You

When It's Your Turn to Complain

Several years ago I was invited to speak at a gathering of Methodist youth ministers in northeast Ohio. I was told I would be leading one workshop on Creative Worship Ideas and then participating in a round-table discussion and Q&A on youth ministry.

When I arrived, I discovered that the people who were hosting the event likely hadn't attended all the meetings of those who had planned the event. The hosts expected me to lead two workshops, the first of which was scheduled to start in two hours.

They asked if I needed anything for the first workshop and, without thinking, I said, "Index cards—lots and lots of index cards." I honestly didn't know what I was going to do with them. I don't even know why I said, "Index cards." Maybe I thought it would force me to focus and come up with something before we arrived at the retreat center.

To begin the workshop, I passed out the index cards "Chap Clark style": I threw them in the air and let the attendees distribute them.

I said, "Write down your biggest complaint about youth ministry and then pass the cards up to me."

Here's a list of what the youth ministers in the crowd came up with:

"Churches only focus on numbers."

"I hate office hours."

"Parents expect you to fix all the problems they created."

"Parents want you to make their kid like them."

"'In-house service project' means 'Come wash the dishes at the spaghetti supper.'"

"Youth are too loud."

"Youth aren't there."

"Youth don't come to service."

"Youth don't behave in service."

"Youth ministers have to be white, bald, goateed, and play guitar."

"I'm expected to be there for everything."

"My mission trip was counted as vacation time."

"Mission trips are EARNED."

"Kids expect me to have all the answers."

"I can't keep up with the kids."

"People keep asking, 'When are you going to be a real minister?'"

"Coaches once respected Sundays."

"If some kids want to go into the mission field to be the hands and feet and eyes and ears and heart of Christ, you don't make them hold a bake sale first."

Okay, those last two came from me.

Do any of those complaints sound familiar? Are there any you'd add to the list? As a youth minister, you have a right to complain. In many churches, youth ministry is an afterthought, at best.

I once worked for a church that quite literally slid a desk into a storage room and said, "Look, we made you an office." That office later became the "resource room," of which I was dubbed "king," even though running the resource room had nothing to do with youth ministry. The church figured, as long as my desk was in there anyway, why not?

You have the right to complain when your job isn't what it's supposed to be. But, as with returning a broken item to the store where you bought it, there's a right way and a wrong way to handle the situation. Let's take a look at the right way.

The Fine Art of Complaining

There's a fine line between making a complaint known and being a complainer. Here are five tips to help you navigate that line:

Step 1: Make sure you're looking at the situation properly.
Does your complaint stand up to scrutiny? If you look at the situation from a different perspective, does your complaint seem petty or minor? Moses' people thought they had a legitimate complaint when they had no meat to eat in the wilderness. They overlooked the fact that they woke up to free breakfast every morning. All they had to do was pick it up from the ground. Ask yourself: If someone gives you free pancakes every morning, do you really want to complain about a lack of bacon?

In order to get an objective view of your complaint, you have to take your ego out of the equation. That's an amazingly difficult thing to do. When people insult what you do or cut your funding or complain about your students, the natural response is to take it personally.

Take a step back and look at the situation objectively. Take your ego out of the equation and see if it's still as big a problem as it was a moment ago. Jesus had critics, too, and *his* nailed him to a piece of wood. You can put up with a few budget cuts.

If you're uncertain about how to take your ego out of the equation, talk to a trusted friend who's not afraid to reach across the table and give you a good old-fashioned dope slap (in a gentle, Christian way, of course). If you can't do that, try shifting positions. Get out of your chair and seat yourself in the "guest chair" (or wherever visitors sit when they come to see you). Visualize yourself behind the desk. Sometimes physically moving to a new spot can help you mentally see a new perspective.

Once you've decided that you have a legitimate complaint and that you're not just suffering from a bruised ego, it's time to make that complaint known.

Step 2: Inform your boss.
You owe your boss the courtesy and respect of letting her know what's going on *before* you take your complaint public. (That is, of course, unless your boss is the one you're complaining about. We'll talk about how to deal with that situation later.) Nothing will hurt your case more than putting your boss in a situation that makes her look like she doesn't know what's happening with her own staff.

I once had a boss who told me, "I really don't like teenagers all that much. What you do on that end of the building is up to you. You're the youth leader. Just don't let me ever be surprised. That's all I ask."

I was able to honor that. I'd call him on Sunday night to say, "Hey, *this* happened, and you might get a visit about it." He'd say, "Okay, thanks for letting me know."

If someone showed up in his office to complain (as often happened), he was prepared—and he always supported me.

Step 3: Be completely clear and honest about what's making you unhappy.

What ticked you off? Was it the way someone treated you? Was it the budget cuts? Was it a lack of support by parents or leaders? Be able to state the problem clearly in your own mind, or you'll never convince anyone else there even *is* a problem.

Step 4: Be completely clear and honest about what you want to happen as a result of your complaint.

Do you want a simple "I'm sorry"? Do you want someone to say, "I was wrong and you were right"? Would you prefer some sort of military tribunal for the person you're angry at? You'll need to be able to state this concisely to the person or committee receiving your complaint.

Step 5: Complain to the right set of ears.

If someone says, "I hate it when Doris gets all possessive about the church kitchen," it's very tempting to say, "Yeah, I know what you mean. One time, she..." If you have a problem with the way

Complaining to a Committee

Unfortunately, sometimes the boss is the source of the problem. No workplace is perfect. No employer or supervisor is perfect. If your denomination has specific guidelines for lodging a complaint against a supervisor, follow those. Respect your boss as a professional (just as you'd want to be respected). Inform the chairman of the board ahead of time that you'll be bringing up certain issues before the board. Let me emphasize: This should be done only *after* you've tried to resolve the problems with your boss on your own...privately.

If your complaint is one that needs to be addressed in a public forum, here are some tips for making the process as smooth and beneficial as possible.

1. First of all, write down your complaint so that you can read it exactly as you intend. If your complaint involves a church member, invite him to the meeting (depending on how your church operates on such matters). State your complaint and your desired

Doris has taken charge of the kitchen, take it up with *Doris*. No one else needs to be involved. Don't publicize your complaint. Ask to meet privately with the person who's upset you. See if the two of you can work it out.

How to Complain to a Parent

Everyone has that little...uh...rascal in his group who seems to go out of his way to disrupt a meeting. Maybe the kid's just "acting out" or maybe he's just a natural-born pain in the posterior. Either way, you have to go to his parents to keep from wringing the kid's neck. How do you approach such a delicate situation?

Here's one of the most valuable ministry tools I've ever learned—one simple sentence that's served me well for nearly 18 years. Ready?

"I need your help with something."

This is the phrase you go to the parents with. A phone call works, but it's often better in person. "I need your help with something. I'm having trouble keeping Jenny from talking during

32

the lesson." Or "I need your help with something. I understand Tom is a totally normal teenage boy with hormones racing through his body, but he's having a problem while at the meetings…"

This simple sentence does many things:

- It shows parents you respect their authority.
- It shows parents that you are not the one who has to "fix" their kid.
- It avoids being an accusation of their parenting skills.
- It creates a dual relationship in the raising of their child.

result calmly. Be open to the committee's ideas. Prepare answers for questions committee members may ask.

2. If possible, walk into the meeting with a list (or diary entries) of the events that led you to your decision. Keep an ongoing record of the people you have squabbles with. If you go into the meeting with a record of the history involved you'll keep the committee from thinking you're flying off the handle.

3. Avoid exaggeration. Don't use words such as "always" and "never." Nothing is "always" or "never."

Six words that will keep arguments to a minimum and may even help solve the problem: "I need your help with something."

Remember, this is your job. You get a check (hopefully). You have the right to expect to be treated a certain way in your workplace. But you can't go off on a rant in front of the wrong people at the wrong time in the wrong place. Offering professional courtesy demonstrates that you're serious about your ministry and that you won't tolerate others trying to diminish it.

Occasionally a well-handled complaint may earn you grudging respect. It may also deflect further complaints from church members who see complaining as a hobby. If repeated attempts to solve the situation go unheeded, it may be time to move on to the next chapter.

Complaints can stick to your soul like the gummy stuff under a price tag. You scrub, rub, even get out a knife to get it all off, but the residue remains. This is the residue that, when it builds up, causes burnout.

Learning the proper way to deal with complaints (yours and others) will keep you around for a long time.

Memorize This

"If we want courteous treatment we have got to see to it that complaints of abusive treatment are made to the proper people." —Mark Twain, "It Pays to Kick"

4. Exit: Stage Left

When It Really *Is* Time to Go

On your feet, sing it with me!!!!

Should I stay or should I go now?
Should I stay or should I go now?
If I go there will be trouble
An' if I stay it will be double
So come on and let me know
Should I stay or should I go?
("Should I Stay or Should I Go?" written by The Clash.
Copyright 1982 by Nineden Limited.)

Some songs are just timeless classics, aren't they? Sometimes we may catch ourselves whistling them while we work. Other times we may find ourselves turning up the volume in the car and screaming along while the windows rattle. I wonder if The Clash ever worked for a church.

Let's start our discussion with one simple phrase:

It's okay to leave.

If no one else has told you that before, I'll tell you now again:

It's okay to leave.

Too many youth workers say, "I hate my job, but I love my kids." Very few youth workers ever leave a job because of their students. Most leave because of administration, parents, the congregation, or their paycheck. And that's okay. It's okay to expect a decent paycheck for the work you do. It's also okay to take time off for the sake of your soul.

But is leaving the right thing for *you* to do *now*, at this point in your ministry? That's the $64,000 question.

Consider This

Every youth worker has a unique tolerance level and a unique set of circumstances surrounding the ministry. The proverbial straw-that-broke-the-camel's-back for one person may be a nonissue for another. Yet anyone facing a crossroads in ministry should consider the following points:

1. Everyone has a limit.

There's an old saying that goes, "Beyond his limit is no place for a man to be." And certainly there are elements of youth ministry that can push a person to the limit—and beyond.

Have you ever tried to carry an armload of socks down a flight of stairs? You drop one, then when you try to pick it up, you drop another. You shift the load a little, and then attempt to pick up the second sock, only to drop two more. Sometimes youth ministry can feel that way.

As youth minister, you have your hands full with the responsibilities of your position. Yet you're also expected to direct the Christmas play, deliver the children's sermon during worship time, shovel the front walk before the first service, or do some other odd jobs. If you're the volunteering type, you may not mind the added workload. But when those tasks start to be expected of you, as if they were part of your job description, they can take a toll. That's why it's important to set your limits early in your job tenure and hold to them.

If you allow yourself to be pushed past your limits in your job, you may find that other areas of your life—your relationship with your spouse and kids and your personal growth, to name just a couple—become as dysfunctional as your job. That's when it's time to reevaluate your position.

2. It is a job.
If you get a paycheck—no matter how small it is—for the work you do, then youth ministry is a job. One of the hardest parts of being a youth minister is knowing where your job ends and your life begins. Congregations have a tendency to treat all ministers as if they were part of the church building. People expect ministers to be accessible 24-7. Don't fall for that line of thinking.

Your church pays you for the work you do. That means you're entitled to time off and the respect that any other organization or company gives its employees.

3. You can have a heart for Jesus and still be fairly compensated.

"Heart for Jesus" is a term that often gets thrown around at salary evaluation time. You start talking about the cost-of-living increase and your financial board starts talking about "having a heart for Jesus." The unspoken expectation is that if you're a servant of God, you've also taken a vow of poverty. The truth is you have the right to be compensated for the work you do.

4. They aren't your kids.

It sounds cruel. It sounds insensitive. It sounds uncaring. But ultimately it's the truth. The kids in your group aren't your children. They have parents. They have teachers. Granted, those adults may not have the relationship with the kids in your group that you do. But if your job is eating you alive, you may have to come to terms with the fact that you can't save the world. God called you to be a youth minister, not the savior of the universe. (He already has that job, and look what they did to him.)

How Do You Know When It's Time to Go?

If you suspect you're nearing your limit in your current position, here are some steps you can take to help you plot your next move:

1. Pray…a lot.

James 1:5-7 in *The Message* puts it this way:

> *If you don't know what you're doing, pray to the Father. He loves to help. You'll get his help, and won't be condescended to when you ask for it. Ask boldly, believingly, without a second thought. People who "worry their prayers" are like*

wind-whipped waves. Don't think you're going to get anything
from the Master that way.

2. Get advice.

God put your friends and family in your life for a reason. God may put complete strangers in your life for a reason. Pick the brains of the people around you. Seek out alternate perspectives on your situation. The book of Proverbs is full of verses about the importance of getting advice from wise counsel:

> "Plans fail for lack of counsel, but with many advisers they succeed." (Proverbs 15:22)

> "If you have good sense, instruction will help you to have even better sense.
> And if you live right, education will help you to know even more." (Proverbs 9:9, CEV)

Think of it in terms of building a coaching staff. Who's your offensive coordinator? Who will give you advice on moving forward? Who are your defensive coaches? Who will give you advice on staying put and sticking it out? Who will break down the numbers for you? Who will tell you whether you can afford to make a move right now?

Who's the team chaplain—the person you can confide in, the one who will help you make the decision with your heart as well as your head?

3. Listen.

I want God to talk to me with a big, flashy neon sign. I want something the size of a building to drop out of the sky, something with giant blinking arrows that point in the direction I'm supposed to go and flashing red and blue lights that spell out THIS WAY!

God doesn't speak to me like that. I want the flashy sign, but what I usually get is a Post-it note. I've had two flashing neon sign moments in my entire life (one I'll tell you about a little later and the other is mine to keep). But I think God puts Post-it notes in front of us all the time.

In 1 Kings 19, Elijah, who's hiding out in a cave, is told God is going to "pass by." Shortly thereafter, God does some cool amusement park special effects with earthquakes and fire. But the Bible tells us that "the LORD was not in the fire" and "the LORD was not in the earthquake."

Then the Bible speaks of a "gentle whisper" that says, "What are you doing here, Elijah?" In other words…"Time to go."

My friend Al says, "God will speak to you in one of two ways. He will whisper in your ear or he will hit you with a brick. Learn to listen for the whisper because the brick hurts. Every time."

4. Don't ask for advice if you're not going to pay attention.
Remember the old joke about the minister who climbs up on the church roof to escape the waters of a massive flood? (It's now been scientifically proved that the joke has been used as a sermon illustration in every church on the planet at least once. Yet congregations *still* pretend to chuckle warmly when the minister trots it out again.)

The joke goes like this: The minister is surrounded by the rising flood waters. A boat comes by and a guy on board calls out, "Time to go, Rev!" But the reverend says, "No, God will take care of me. Go west about a mile. Mrs. Murphy is probably stuck in her house." So the boat leaves.

The waters continue to rise. Another boat comes along and a man calls out, "Time to go, Rev!" But the minister says, "No, God will take care of me. Mrs. Howver has six kids, and I'm sure they're all frightened. Go help them." So the boat leaves.

As the water level gets higher and higher, a helicopter arrives, hovers over the church roof and lowers its ladder. But the minister waves it off, shouting, "God will take care of me. Have you evacuated the nursing home yet?" So the chopper leaves.

A short while later, the water level rises above the church building and the minister drowns. Standing before the Lord, he asks, "God, why didn't you take care of me?"

"What are you talking about?" God replies. "I sent you two boats and a helicopter!"

For a biblical spin on the same theme, check out this (liberally embellished) story from 2 Chronicles 18:

Ahab, the king of Israel, said to Jehoshaphat, the king of Judah, "I'm going to attack Ramoth Gilead. Wanna come and bring some guys with you?"

And, lo, did Jehoshaphat say unto him, "Sure. But let's ask God for guidance first."

So the king of Israel gathered 400 preachers and teachers and asked, "What does God think of this little road trip we're planning?"

The preachers and the teachers said, "Bring it on."

But, lo, Jehoshaphat was a wuss and spake, saying, "Is there another prophet around we could ask?"

Ahab, the king of Israel, said, "Yeah, there's a guy named Micaiah, but I don't like what he tells me. He's so negative all the time."

Jehoshaphat said, "You shouldn't bad-mouth your preacher."

Ahab replied, "Yeah? How long have you been doing church work?" (No, I'm just kidding. The king said, "Okay, we'll listen, we'll listen.")

While they waited, the 400 preachers and teachers put on a play directed by somebody's wife.

When Micaiah showed up, the king asked him, "So? Should we stay or should we go?"

Micaiah said, "I wouldn't go."

Ahab said, "That's it? No song and dance? No poetry?"

So Micaiah put the whole thing into a nifty performance piece and said that God was pretty fed up with Ahab and wanted to get him to attack Ramoth Gilead and be killed. So God sent an angel to whisper in the ears of the 400 prophets and got them all to tell one big, collective fib.

The king said to Jehoshaphat, "See? What'd I tell you? Always with the gloom and doom, this guy."

So the king had Micaiah arrested and ordered he be put in chains until the king returned from the war.

Micaiah replied, "Yeah, there's goes my retirement."

But just before the battle, Ahab, the king of Israel, said to Jehoshaphat, "Here, you wear my robe and I'll put on this common soldier's armor, and then we can go into battle."

Meanwhile, back at the ranch, the king of Aram ordered his troops to shoot only the king.

The battle commenced. Aram's soldiers grabbed the man in the king's robes, but then realized they had the wrong guy, so they let him go.

During the battle a stray arrow found its way into a little space in Ahab's armor. The wounded king was removed from the battle and died later that night.

As Bugs Bunny would say, "What a maroon!"

If you ask God for advice…and God gives it to you…and you ignore it…you're going to have a problem.

5. Look before you leap.
"Is there anyone here who, planning to build a new house, doesn't first sit down and figure the cost so you'll know if you can complete it?" (Luke 14:28, *The Message*).

Leaving your position is not a decision to make on the spur of the moment. You can't get angry at your job review or at a board meeting and storm out the door. At least, not if you expect to get hired somewhere else.

Before you make a move, look for open doors. If you truly feel in your soul that it's time for you to go, then somewhere there's a door opening for you. God will not leave you idle for long.

However, while God *will* open the door for you, he will not push you through it. It's up to *you* to cross the threshold. On that stormy night on the Sea of Galilee, Jesus didn't sit next to Peter in the boat and say, "Go." Jesus stood out on the water and said, "Come."

The decision to step out of the boat rests solely with you.

6. You work according to God's timing, not yours.
Being a servant of God means going where you're sent, when he sends you. It could be that the purpose for your being where you are now has been accomplished. Perhaps without your even

realizing it. You may only recognize that purpose years from now, in retrospect.

I have a friend who worked for a certain church for a very short time, even by youth ministry standards. During his short tenure there, he had a young man in the youth group whose father had left the family just three weeks before the youth minister started. My friend mentored the young man through his senior year. Just three weeks after the young man graduated, the youth minister was let go.

"I didn't see it then," my friend recalled. "I didn't see it until years later. I said, 'God, I'm your servant,' and God put me in that church for that reason. I don't want to think about what would have happened to that kid if I weren't there. That job was hell on earth, but at least now I know why I was there."

7. Don't look back.

There's a strange little story by Stephen King called *The Langoliers*. It involves a group of travelers who are caught in the past—not the distant past, but the past as in 15 minutes ago. The travelers are alone in the world because they exist 15 minutes after everyone else. (I know how weird it sounds, but it's a Stephen King story—and he explains it better.)

The problem is that the past eventually vanishes. It becomes nothing. And the group of travelers who find themselves living in the past have to get back to the present before they vanish along with the rest of reality. (The Langoliers turn out to be little scary monsters that eat away at the fabric of time. I'll avoid any insensitive comparisons to your administrative board.)

Once you make your decision to leave, you can't look behind you. It's in the past. And it will slowly disappear. You have to keep moving forward. You set your plan. You made your decision. Now start walking.

Going back to Peter in the boat, his step over the edge was his defining moment. After that venture onto the water, he could never be the same again. He could only move forward.

When you make a decision, you usually have choices, right? Boxers or briefs. Coke or Pepsi. Left or right. Stay or go. Once you make your decision, you have to give up the other choice. You don't get both.

Once you make your decision, you must follow it. If you decide to go, you have to give up on everything that would have resulted by staying. Trying to hold on to the past is unhealthy.

If you decide to leave your job, you probably shouldn't attend the graduation ceremony of the seniors in your old group. That's your past. You are their past. All of you need to move on. This is perhaps the hardest part about making the decision to leave.

Are you in this for the long haul? Are you going to be one of those really old people walking around the National Youth Workers Convention? Are you planning to progress from being the Luke Skywalker of youth ministry to the Obi-Wan? The Yoda? If so, it's a guarantee that sometime during your career you're going to have to walk out the door. It's painful. But sometimes the Potter may use a church or a group of people to mash you against the wheel so you can survive the fire later on.

Memorize This
Sometimes that light at the end of the tunnel
is an EXIT sign.

5. Getting Fired for the Glory of God[1]

When Leaving Isn't Your Idea

Many of you will read this chapter and remember when you were fired. Others of you will read this chapter and think, "I hope that never happens to me."

Mike Yaconelli once wrote, "I'm beginning to believe that if those who are called to youth ministry follow the lead of the One who called them, getting fired is inevitable."

Most of you who are in this for the long haul will probably be fired from your church job at some point in your career.

Have you ever been to a student's home and noticed a family portrait on the mantel? The whole family is smiling and looking happy, but you know that kid and you know the things that have come up in your counseling sessions. You know that those smiles are as fake as the plastic "wood" frame the portrait hangs in. Churches are like that.

The church is supposed to be a place of unconditional love and acceptance. The result is that people who are running from

[1] This title was taken from an article by Mike Yaconelli.

dysfunction run to the church—and bring their dysfunction with them. Some of those dysfunctional people may be on the board that hired you.

We all have our baggage. Some of us have steamer trunks. Some of us have one of those shiny little gold purses. Some of us have steamer trunks and *think* we have shiny little gold purses. We are accepted in the church. Like Jesus, the church loves us for who we are. Unfortunately, sometimes "who we are" is a person with problems, and when those people rise to positions of authority in the church they often lead from the baggage claim area and not from the pilot seat.

I was fired twice—well, technically, I was fired only once. The other time the board discovered that the amount of the budget deficit was almost exactly the same as my salary, so "my contract was not renewed." (But, yeah, I was fired.)

As for my "official" firing, I thought long and hard about telling you the story of what happened and what was said. But I decided that would be self-serving. Instead, I'll wait a bit and tell you another story about why I'm still in this business.

Losing Your Job Is Not That Different from Losing a Loved One

As youth workers, we put our hearts and souls into our jobs. That's part of what makes us good at them. It's also what keeps us at our jobs long after we should have left.

When that relationship is taken away, it can feel like a death.

Most counselors point to the five stages of grief when they talk about healing from the death of a loved one. In the case of a fired youth worker, "death" is a separation from a group of kids that you loved like your own. As a result, you may experience some or all of those five stages of grief:

1. Denial

I've known several youth ministers who lost their jobs and immediately started holding Bible studies in their own house or a local coffee shop with their former students. That kind of situation can never turn out good. When a loved one dies, it's natural to want to stay with the body or spend hours and hours at the cemetery talking to a headstone. But life stops when you do that. You can't bring back a loved one who's died by pretending it didn't happen. And you can't change the fact that you were fired by spending time with your former group.

To continue a relationship with your former students is detrimental to you and to them. When I was fired, it took me a long time to stop thinking of the group in my former church as "my kids." It occurred to me later that I was only making it harder for myself to move on. Once you accomplish what God put you in a specific place to do, you have to be willing to be obedient when God tells you it's time to move on.

If you're still in the picture, it will make things much harder for the new youth worker who comes into the situation with her own agenda, her own gifts, her own talents. She needs to be able to do *her* job, not take over and do *your* job. There's a certain amount of professional courtesy that must be shown when you leave a church.

2. Anger

When I was fired, I wasn't the only member of the staff to be let go. A number of us were bounced together. One staff member took it especially hard. She sat down with the membership directory and began calling church members to tell them her side of the story. Whether she was hoping to elicit support or make the administrators of the church look bad, I don't know. She was angry and fueled a fire that had been burning for a long time. The frustrations and stress she'd been keeping buried deep inside suddenly came spewing out like venom. The result was that she wound up alienating herself from those who might have been sympathetic to her.

To rage about your church in front of your students would be even worse. A student of mine who graduated a year or so after I was fired called me up and invited me to lunch. I spent the first part of the meal unloading anger I'd been bottling up without realizing it. The experience was painful to her and painful to me.

Anger is normal. What you do with it is up to you. You can channel that anger into energy and use it to get another position.

You can also give it to God. (God's been given a great deal of anger because he deals with it better than we do.) Visualize your anger. What does it look like? Dog food? Coal? Snakes? Whatever it looks like, use your imagination to box it up. Wrap it in duct tape. Visualize yourself giving it to God—and visualize yourself letting it go. (Sometimes I had dreams that I was sneaking into this giant warehouse—like the one in the end of *Raiders of the Lost Ark*—and stealing my anger back.)

Read Job 38. Job has just finished unloading on God and now God says, in effect "Sit down, Junior. We're going to talk."

Dealing with your anger takes time. You're not going to get over it tomorrow. Give yourself permission to be angry. Then give yourself permission to let it go.

3. Bargaining

I can't tell you the number of times I asked God to give me a clue—to give me just a hint—as to what "the big picture" was. I was willing to accept that I was fired, but I was unwilling to accept that it was part of a bigger plan. I loved those kids and could not, for the life of me, understand how leaving them could be the work of God.

I demanded answers. I got empty air. I spent a lot of time angry at God. Didn't I go where I was told? Didn't I do what he wanted? Why would he send me someplace if I was just going to get fired less than two years later? I was angry at God, and when God didn't answer me the way *I* decided God should, I took the anger out on people who loved me.

4. Depression

When you lose your job, especially a church job, it's easy to get depressed. It's easy to turn away not only from the work but also from the church and from God. You start to wrestle with the question, "What's the point?"

One of the most bizarre movies I've ever seen (and a personal favorite of mine) is *From Dusk Till Dawn*. In it, Harvey Keitel plays a minister who's lost his faith. (He finds it again near the end of the movie with one of my favorite lines from a clergy in all of film history.) In an early scene, which takes place at a little roadside diner, he tries to explain what he's going through to his daughter. "What I am experiencing is closer to an awakening," he says. "There is not a monk, a rabbi, a nun, or a minister who does not look at himself in the mirror at one time and say, 'Am I a fool?'"

Losing your job in the church can make you question everything you believe—and that uncertainty can send you into a spiral of depression.

5. Acceptance

This step took a long time for me. For months, when my new boss would say, "We're doing job reviews next week," I would go into a panic. I would walk into the meeting ready to angrily justify myself and my actions to anyone who dared to question them. Even when I was long gone from the church, the sting of being fired stuck with me. Eventually, though, you will say in prayer, "Okay, what's next?" and you will mean it—for God's purposes and not your own.

Of course, saying to God, "Okay, I'm ready to move on," isn't going to get you very far if God knows perfectly well that you are, in fact, *not* ready to move on. God's timing is perfect. When you're ready to move on, God will be there to guide you.

But how do you reach that point? Mark Twain once said, "The best way to cheer yourself up is to cheer somebody else up."

You're in ministry. You need to be out with the people. During the time I was out of my youth ministry job, I got "seasonal" employment at a toy store. (I was on Elmo Security.) I also worked the floor and was named employee of the month my first month there. It was an easy ministry ("What do you need?" "I have that right here." "I can get that for you.") But it fulfilled something inside me. It also allowed me to work without politics or administrative boards.

Eventually you'll get to the point where you can say, "Okay, God, what am I supposed to be learning here?" You can't force this one. You have to realize it. Ask God in prayer, "What is it you want me to learn?" If all you get is "empty air," that doesn't mean you're being ignored. It means maybe you're not ready yet. It means maybe the next step of your life isn't ready yet, so you get a chance to chill and cool off and then move on.

Remember my friend in chapter 4? He didn't know why God had put him in that church for such a short time until long after he left. Once you can get past "What am I supposed to learn?" then you can move on.

Looking back on it, I see how my own prayers changed in the months between ministry gigs. Here's a recap:
DENIAL: Why me, God?
ANGER: Why aren't you helping me?
BARGAINING: I need a new ministry job, God. Now. Please.
DEPRESSION: Forget it. I'm outta here.
ACCEPTANCE: I am your servant.

Servant
This is the last piece that goes into the puzzle after getting fired.

In the 17th century, a monk named Brother Lawrence believed he'd found the secret to feeling connected to God all the time. Many of his writings and letters were collected in the book *The Practice of the Presence of God* (reworked for a new generation under the title *God Is Here* by Steve Case).

Once, during a stay in a monastery, Brother Lawrence was accused of a crime against his fellow monks. He doesn't write about what the accusation was. We know only that the charges were proved to be false. But when he was first confronted with them and with the threat of being kicked out of the monastery, Brother Lawrence said only, "If I cannot serve God here, I will serve him elsewhere."

He didn't defend himself. He didn't ask for proof. He said, "If not here, then someplace else."

When you say, "God, I am your servant," God will take you up on the offer. He's the one who said, "I have plans for you. I have plans to make you prosper and not to harm you. I have plans to give you hope for the future" (Jeremiah 29:11, author's paraphrase).

And remember what Bruno (of the band Bruno and the Heaters) said: "Whatever don't kill you makes you stronger."[2]

As I wrap up this chapter, let me tell you the story of why I'm still in youth ministry.

One day while I was out of work, I was listening to the radio and I heard that Geoff Moore (when he was still with The Distance) was going to be at a local Christian bookstore.

[2] Some have attributed this quote to Nietzsche.

By that time I'd decided I was officially done with youth ministry. I believed that God was telling me, "Okay, that's it. Thanks for your time. Good job. Now bye-bye." I was checking the want ads for jobs in advertising and radio (what I'd done before going into youth ministry). I was convinced that I'd put in my time and now was done.

I went to the bookstore to await the arrival of Mr. Moore and one or two of his bandmates. Neither the store nor the station had done a spectacular job of promoting the event. Only about five people had shown up. As I said, I was sure I was done with youth ministry, but I wanted to tell Mr. Moore how much his music had meant to my ministry when I was still doing it.

He arrived and shook a few hands. He talked with other people while I waited. Eventually I made my way over and introduced myself. I said I really liked his music and told him it had meant a lot to my ministry.

He said, "What church are you working for now?"

Well, for some reason, I thought that was an invitation to unload my life story and tell him how I was no longer with the church and how I'd decided God was telling me to move on and do something else.

He waited patiently while I unloaded. I still don't know why he did that. He could have said, "Oh, well, good luck. Bye." But he listened to me until I was done. Then he picked up a copy of his new disc and signed it. He handed it to me and said, "Don't go. We need you."

That was it. That was all he needed to say. "Don't go. We need you."

In chapter 4, we talked about signs. God will give them to you. I believe—no, I *know*—that God used Geoff Moore at that moment and put him in my life to say, "Don't go. We need you."

I'm still here.

Memorize This
There's a reason they call it FIRED. It burns.
It also makes you stronger.

6. Do Not Ride This Ride If You Have Back Trouble or a Heart Condition

When You Feel Like You're Getting Too Old for This Stuff

Deep in the heart of upper northeast Ohio, there's an amusement park—'scuse me, an "AMAZE-ment" park—called Cedar Point. Known to roller coaster enthusiasts everywhere, Cedar Point has more coasters than any other park in the world. It also touts some of the fastest and tallest wooden coasters and metal monsters.

I used to love to go there. Once a year, the park would have "Youth Group Day," in which youth groups in our denomination within a 100-mile radius or so would descend on the park and run from one end to the other all day long. (Then some people, in their infinite Christian wisdom, decided it would be a good idea to have worship services during Youth Group Day. That meant we had to get out of line, run back to the park entrance and sit in an un-air-conditioned auditorium to sing about God's love for 45 minutes. It was enough to make the teenagers question whether God really loved them.)

Several years after I become a youth minister, I gathered my groups together and made the trip to Cedar Point. As we walked up to the gate, I could feel the kids practically vibrating. They were ready to explode. I tried to keep them together long enough to pick our meeting spot when it was time to go home.

We paired them up. We set a meeting time (on the blue bench in front of the ice cream stand at 10:30), and I let them go. Have you ever seen one of those Road Runner cartoons where the Coyote is standing with something in his hand, ready to ambush the Road Runner, only to have the Road Runner zip by and leave him standing empty-handed? That's what it was like when the kids took off. Bang. Zoom. Gone.

The other adults and I were left standing there in the breeze caused by the mass evacuation of students who were there one moment and then simply were…not.

After the kids left, we adults got out our maps and talked about which rides would be most popular and how we could avoid them in the middle of the day when the sun was hottest. We decided to do the new roller coasters in the morning and then hit the giant movie screen attraction in the afternoon because it was air-conditioned and we could sit down—and maybe get a cookie.

In the middle of the discussion, my friend Doug and I looked at each other and said simultaneously, "You're old."

I used to *run* the park. And there I was, studying the map and planning my day around air-conditioning and getting a cookie. If you stay in youth ministry long enough, you get old. Your students already perceive you that way, of course, but eventually you'll start to see yourself as old as well.

The Myth of the Midlife Crisis

When a boy is 16, he wants a cherry-red convertible, or perhaps a sports car—something hot, something with speed, something that looks like it would fly if he could just get it to a runway and off the street with the school-crossing sign.

But, of course, the boy can't afford such a pleasure. He may be able to purchase something for a few hundred bucks—something that rattles and shimmies, something he'll spend hours waiting for in the shop or working on under the hood, wondering how to disconnect the what's-it from the framinator.

The boy goes off to college. The beater can't make the long drive, so perhaps the boy borrows a grand from his dad to buy something that will get him to and from campus. It looks nothing like the cherry-red convertible of his dreams, but it's a car and that's enough for now.

He meets a nice young lady. She's sweet and thinks his car is cute, and they fall in love. When they graduate college and move into the real world, she tells him he needs something more respectable if he's going to be a professional. He ditches his campus babe magnet and buys something he can afford on his limited salary. No convertible yet. After all, he has to start saving for a ring and a family and get his retirement account going.

After he gets married, he finds himself struggling to get the baby seat in the back of the sensible car he bought when he got out of college. He realizes he has only one option. He'll be lucky if the new minivan is red. He'll settle for blue, as long as it doesn't have the wood-grain panel down the side.

He drives the minivan for years, and then trades it in for a cooler minivan when the kids reach junior high. After that, he has to get serious about saving for college, so all plans for new cars are put on hold indefinitely.

The kids graduate college. They get jobs, spouses, and lives and salaries of their own. Finally our hero finds himself at the top of his game. He's well paid. He has a loving spouse. His bills are under control. He's finally able to look at that hot-rod magazine he's had since his teens. He ventures to the dealership and, at age 50, our 16-year-old teenage boy drives off the lot with the car of his dreams.

And gets laughed at. "Oh, look, George is going through his midlife crisis!"

Hey, You're Middle-Aged!

What is middle-aged? Take the age at which you die and cut it in half. That's when you're middle-aged. Oh...you want to talk about when the rest of the world has decided you are middle-aged? Okay, we can do that. One of the hardest parts of being middle-aged is actually seeing yourself that way.

A few years back, I met the son of an old friend and I realized how much he looked like his old man did when we were teenagers. Then I realized how much my friend now looked like his own dad. It also occurred to me that I was the proverbial "friend of Dad's." I was lumped in with all the "grown-ups." In my heart I wanted to hang out with the son because he was "my age"—or at least the age that I saw myself.

At the last family Christmas celebration I attended, my cousin brought her daughters and my brother brought his son. As I looked around the room, I realized we were the exact same family as when I was a child, sitting on the floor wondering when we were going to open presents. Only now, my parents were the grandparents and my cousin's daughters and my nephew were in the little kid role I used to have. I was now the 40-ish uncle who made sarcastic comments and got shirts as gifts instead of toys.

We look at teenagers and marvel at their devil-may-care attitudes and their occasionally dangerous behavior. We attribute them to the fact that "teenagers think they're going to live forever." And from the teenager's perspective, it's true. They're going to live for so many more years they don't have a concept of it all coming to an end. When you're middle-aged, you frequently get heavy doses of perspective that can be frightening.

You start to take stock of issues in your life that you haven't had to consider before. You worry more about your health. You no longer have a metabolism that can digest Tupperware.

There's an important question that you didn't ask when you were a baby: "What am I going to do with the next 40 years of my life?" When you're young, there's only "now." This is now. Back then? That's not now. Now is now. Five minutes from now? That's not now. That's five minutes from now. Now is now.

When you're middle-aged, "now" is part of "then." "Then" helped shaped "now." Then is part of now. Now is also part of "when." Everything you do now affects "when." Then. Now. When. All are linked when you reach middle age.

Let's Do the Time Warp Again

We recently ordered my daughter's senior pictures. She is tall and slim and beautiful. We're looking into scholarship programs and colleges. The other day, as I was carefully cutting the white part away from the page of wallet-sized photos of her senior picture, she called to me from the other room, "Dad, look what I found!"

In her hand was a photo of her and her little brother and me. It was taken on her first day of first grade and my son's first day of kindergarten. The photo shows me with one kid sitting on each arm. It's a harsh awakening to realize you're no longer the guy with the dark hair and the kids sitting on your arms.

That was just yesterday, right? I remember it clearly. It couldn't have been more than a week ago.

Aw, enough of that.

Right now, most of your students are thinking that time is all but standing still. They feel as if they're moving in slow motion. They want to get past this stage of life so badly they could explode.

You're probably thinking that time is moving too quickly. You see a new crop of kids and think, "I was there when that kid got baptized—when he barfed on the minister. Now he's in my youth group?"

Like Making the Perfect Hoagie and Not Eating It

One of the great disadvantages of youth ministry is that we seldom see the fruits of our labor. Most of our young people are with us for four short years (maximum), and then they're off to college. Combine that with the relatively short time many people stay in youth ministry, and we're left with a continuous sense of "Whatever happened to...?"

> "So that you may live a life worthy of the Lord and please him in every way: bearing fruit in every good work, growing in the knowledge of God."
> (Colossians 1:10)

The good news is that if you stick it out long enough as a youth worker, your former students start to come back. When they become adults, many of them will say, "Do you remember when you _____? That really meant a lot to me."

I once gave a graduating student a thesaurus in which I'd gone through and highlighted words like *integrity*, *patience*, and *kindness*. A few years later I got a call at two o'clock in the morning from that student. He was working on a term paper and had found the word *perseverance* highlighted in yellow as he was looking for something else. He called me just to say, "Thank you."

Those are the moments you live for when you're in youth ministry. The longer you stick it out, the more of those amazing moments you'll have. After nearly 20 years in youth ministry, I've had three students go into some sort of ministry themselves. I have a picture of one of my students with a group of his students. There's no way to accurately describe how that feels.

Bring It On
Experience is the best teacher. If you don't believe that, read Psalm 27. Go ahead. Dog-ear this page and go look up Psalm 27.

That's the voice of experience talking. The title of the psalm may as well have been "Bring It On."

Every complainer who comes to your door…

Every negative job review you receive…

Every committee that forms to rework the job description based on the "failings" of the last youth worker…just makes you a little better at what you do.

Whatever don't kill you…

I went through some amazingly bad churches in 20 years. Committees were formed and people met in secret to discuss ways to get rid of me. I was fired in a mean, nasty, and unprofessional way. But those things gave me an armor—a chest plate over my soul with a big red "S" on it, a shield that causes bullets to bounce right off.

Read Psalm 118:6. Read it out loud. Read it like you're indestructible. "Ha! I work for God. What can these mere mortals do to me?"

Well, they can fire you, but they can't kill you. Now, when I hear complaints about my ministry, I think, "Phe, puny human."

In the words of the band Lost and Found: "Oh, them lions, they can eat my body but they can't swallow my soul." (In a moment we'll hear more from one of the band members.)

A Plan Is in Place

Eventually every youth minister in his 40s (or older) looks around and says, "Is this something a grown person should be doing for a living?" You're still sleeping on an air mattress, taking kids on mission trips, eating dangerous amounts of junk food, and laughing at fart jokes that would amuse a 12-year-old.

Is that really where God wants you to be?

Are you kidding? The answer is yes. That's exactly where God wants you to be. In this author's humble opinion, there is no higher calling than youth ministry.

People love working in the nursery. In the nursery you get hugs and smiles, and your students actually act like they're glad to see you.

People like working with adults because you can have conversations that don't include a sharp turn into the topic of gas.

Teenagers, however, terrify the average churchgoer. If you're working with teenagers, you're where God wants you to be. Why? Because God has a plan.

George Baum, cofounder of the band Lost and Found, tells his own story of what happened when he was wondering what to do with the second 40 years of his life.

So one day when I was about 40, I went to my Episcopalian priest and said, "I'd like to take some classes in theology. Where do you recommend I go to do that?" He said, "Well, it depends on whether you want to be ordained or not."

Since I was perfectly happy in my current career, I had no desire to make some drastic switch to being a priest. However, I told him I would pray about ordination and get back to him. I was ambivalent over whether or not I was called in this direction. Thus, I threw myself into the Discernment Process, expecting that when it came time to discern the external call, I would be diverted back to my original goal: Taking some classes in theology. You know, humor the priest and then get back on with living my very enjoyable life.

Well, to make a long story short, the diversion never came. In trusting my future to the process, I eventually found that The Process had a more interesting future for me. So, now I'm two years into seminary. I am still continuing with my old career of playing in a band, and expect to continue that for years to come. So in some odd way, it's as though I've taken out a second mortgage on my life.

Having sold our house and most of our possessions, we don't know where we're headed, but we are trusting, as Paul writes in Philippians, that the one who began a good work in us will bring it to completion by the day of Jesus Christ.

Perhaps the greatest example of God using someone who was getting on in years was Simeon, in Luke 2. God told Simeon that he would not die before he saw the Christ child.

Simeon was one old guy. He sat outside the temple and waited for the day when God would fulfill his purpose. God could have chosen a younger person to greet Mary, Joseph, and the baby Jesus at the temple. But God chose Simeon. He used Simeon's gifts and then allowed him to hold the Messiah in his arms. It was all part of the plan.

Here's a quick test for you: Check your pulse. Go ahead. Got one? Guess what? You're not done yet.

Portions of this very chapter were written a day after the author spent the night in the Washington Dulles Airport in DC. I was on my way back from a conference and had a 50-minute layover in Washington. The screen in the terminal said, "Delayed." My 11:59 departure became 2:45, then 3:30. Then, as I was talking on the phone to my wife, I watched as each individual flight on the screen flipped from Delayed to Canceled...Canceled... Canceled...Canceled.

A mass of bodies ran to the customer service counter. I was about 300 people away from the counter, with about 400 or more people behind me. My wife worked frantically from our home computer to get me on another flight. Soon thereafter, I was booked on a 6:30 a.m.(!) flight. The nearest hotel that still had rooms available and offered an airport shuttle was $250 a night. It was going to be the cleaning crew and me at Dulles.

I bought a sandwich and quizzed the guy behind the counter about airport accommodations. He told me the area between Gates C and D had the best sleeping benches—no armrest dividers.

At two o'clock I was listening to someone on the PA system repeatedly call for Jacques somebody-or-other to return to the gate, a well-meaning cleaning woman sing hymns in Spanish (loudly, to hear herself over her vacuum cleaner), and Headline News anchors alternately talking about the war and the Anna Nicole Smith hearings.

I decided I was profoundly too old for this stuff.

Even the Lone Ranger Had a Tonto

Read Acts 16:1-3. Remember when Moses said to God, "I can't do that. I'm not good enough"? God said, "Fine. Take somebody with you." In the Acts passage, God gave Timothy to Paul. (Probably not his first choice as an assistant, but Paul took what he could get.)

Starting to feel a little burned out? Get an assistant. Find a volunteer within the congregation. Contact your local college or seminary for a list of students who would love some actual youth ministry experience. Recruit some of your graduated seniors to work with you in the junior high meetings.

Yes, God called you to youth ministry, but it's doubtful that he called you to do it alone. In addition to being able to pass off some of the work to someone who actually *has* energy, you have the opportunity to pass on the benefits of your experience as well. You have all the been-there-done-that wisdom. What you don't have is the time, gas, and energy to pick up all the stuff you're going to need for the lock-in pizza party and get all the permission slips signed.

One of the benefits of getting older is being able to share your experience with someone else. And that brings us to our final point.

A Season for Everything There Is, Hmmmmmmm?

I had just started at a new church. One of the first things on the calendar I had to pick up and run with was a Winter Retreat. Apparently the tradition at the Winter Retreat was a Saturday morning pancake breakfast. Eager to make a good impression on students and chaperones, I accepted the challenge of a young man who claimed he could eat more pancakes than I could. I was a little more than twice his age at the time.

He ate 17 pancakes.

I ate 15 pancakes. Temporarily. Unfortunately, all 15 of them decided to make a sudden "reappearance for Jesus." Age and experience count for nothing sometimes.

Let's put this age issue in sci-fi geek terms.

You can be Luke Skywalker. You can swing over chasms, pull out the blaster and fire randomly, and jump into adventure with an enthusiasm only someone new to the game can possess.

You can be Obi-Wan Kenobi. You can pursue adventure with the perspective of someone who's done it before. You can give the "Lukes" of this world guidance and protection. With a simple phrase you can disarm guards, calm a situation, and strike a bargain when you need a spaceship (or at least a 15-passenger van). Having "been there, done that" gives you the responsibility of guiding those who have never done this before.

I was a relative newbie to youth ministry when I attended my very first Youth Specialties National Youth Workers Convention. I had about four years under my belt. I remember that Tic Long took the stage and had everyone stand up. He told us to sit down when he named the number of years we'd been in youth ministry.

He started to count: 1...2...3...4. I sat.

5...6...7...8...9. More than half the people in the room were sitting by that time.

Eventually Tic got up to 40...41...42. There were two people left standing.

43...44...45. The second-to-last person sat down, leaving a lone woman standing in the back of the room. Tic called out, "How many years?"

She called back, "47!"

The entire room of about 4,000 workers erupted. We spontaneously leaped to our feet and gave her a standing ovation. We later learned that the woman had spent 47 years in youth ministry AS A VOLUNTEER!

In the second round, Tic counted in the opposite direction, trying to find the person with the least experience on the job. A young man near the front who'd been in youth ministry for only two months took that title. Youth Specialties bought both people dinner at the hotel restaurant.

The longer you stay in this business, the more opportunity you have to share your experiences and knowledge with those who are just starting out.

In addition to the Luke Skywalkers and Obi-Wan Kenobis, there are a few Yodas in youth ministry. Not many, but a few. Yoda did a lot of observing. He offered advice and tutelage. He knew the right time to speak and the right thing to say. And when no one else believed that miracles were possible, Yoda lifted the X-wing fighter out of the swamp.

Memorize This
Just because there's snow on the roof doesn't mean there's no fire in the furnace. (In fact, snow on the roof means there's good insulation and the heating bills won't dip into the kids' college fund.)

7. Religion and the Pomophobic Church

Or, Fear and Loathing in the Board Meeting

Pomophobic (po-mo-FO-bic):

1. *The fear of postmodern theology.*
2. *The fear of anything or anyone having to do with change.*

The First United Methodist Church of Howverville says "debts" instead of "trespasses."

All Faith Episcopal no longer uses wine for communion; they're using red cranberry juice.

First Light UCC has an openly gay senior pastor.

Little Creek Family Church (which split off from Big River, which split off from Swan Lake) is preaching that there is no hell and that "heaven" and "the Kingdom of God" are two different things.

Does anybody remember when our biggest arguments were with people of other religions? Now it seems we'll fight to the death with people in another pew.

When it comes right down to it, yeah, those people in the new contemporary service really are trying to take over the church, burn the hymnals, and force everyone over 60 out the door. There, does that feel better?

There was a time when people in the congregation weren't allowed to read Scripture. Bibles were provided to priests, who had the final say on what texts were or were not read from the pulpit. As we've grown in our faith (and I use "we" to refer to all Christians everywhere), we've begun to take advantage of our freedom to choose. "Church shopping" is perfectly acceptable. If you don't like the church you're in, or if the pastor says something you disagree with, you can worship at the church down the street.

Church shopping is something that used to happen only when a person moved to another city. A survey of the silver-haired members of your congregation would probably reveal that many of them have been members for 20, 30, maybe even 50 years.

What happened to tradition? People could go to a church for the comfort of knowing who was going to be there and which hymns would be sung. When life got chaotic, the church was our rock, our foundation. It was something we could count on.

Many people in the congregation today think of themselves as an audience, not a part of the service. They think they're in church to be sung to and prayed for. The sermon is like a movie to them.

Nondenominational churches are growing faster in number than denominational churches. Change is one of the most uncomfortable things a church can go through. Unfortunately, to solve this problem, many churches have decided not to change—ever.

In many churches, youth ministry is synonymous with change. That's why so many churches go through youth workers so quickly.

Picture a vast chasm. In the center is a small piece of land. (Imagine an old Road Runner cartoon where the Coyote has survived a bomb blast and is standing on a spot of ground with emptiness on all sides.) Others stand on the edge of the chasm and try to toss a rope or build a bridge to the center, but their offers of help are refused. In fact, if this is all there is to stand on, those who are standing on it will fight harder and harder to keep it, even as it crumbles around them.

When you read that last paragraph, did you picture yourself as the one tossing a lifeline to the last one stuck in the crumbling tradition? Most of us want to think of ourselves as the one on the other side of the chasm. Too often, though, we don't know we're the ones fighting a losing battle. Too often the battles are occurring within the walls of our own church.

I was the last person I know to get a cell phone. I hate cell phones. I've seen people eat lunch with friends while talking on a cell phone. I've seen drivers screaming on their cell phones while weaving back and forth in traffic. I refused to get one. Eventually I discovered that I was the deterrent to communication. My refusal to stay up to date, my decision to fight for the little piece of land I had in that chasm, became a problem for my ministry.

For many, the church is our second home. It's our second family. We don't like anyone coming in and making changes.

"I like my hymns in the book in front of me. I don't need to read the words off the wall."

"Communion is Wonder Bread and wine. Why would we switch to grape juice?"

"Worship is at 8:30. Not 9:30 and not 10:00. If people can't get out of bed to get to church, then maybe they shouldn't stay out so late on Saturday night."

If we're going to survive, we're going to change. The more I dig in my heels, the more ground I lose.

Maybe you aren't the one in the middle. Maybe you're the one on the other side tossing the lifeline. If so, don't be surprised if the offer is refused. If all the person has left is a little tiny piece of land, he's going to fight even harder to keep it.

Can't We All Just Get Along?

How do we try to please people who will never see Mountain Dew and finger darts (aka. finger rockets) as tools for ministry? How do we explain that hand motions are not just for vacation Bible school anymore—and that we call them "sacred movement" now? How can we get past the differences that separate us not only from the church across the street but also from the person across the aisle?

I attended a recent gathering at a conference center in the southern part of the country. The conference drew about 900 young people and youth ministers from a mainline denomination. Sharing the center that weekend were attendees of a couples retreat sponsored by some of our more conservative brothers and sisters in Christ.

I was hanging out at the registration table. (Usually that's the place where you find the people with the best sense of humor and the most patience, two things that are required when you're dealing with someone like me.) A gentleman from the couples retreat came over to talk. We thought he was going to complain about the noise level, but what he wanted to do was tell us that the way we believed was wrong. He started with the idea that we "allowed" (his word, not mine) "our women" (again, his words) to wear pants. He went on from there.

Keep in mind I'm not a member of the particular denomination that hosted the conference. I slip even further to the left than they like to lean. To have this gentleman tell the organizers of the event they were simply wrong in the way they were ministering to young people was, in my opinion, deplorable behavior. Here we had the grand opportunity to learn from each other, share with each other and, as God said through the prophet Isaiah, "reason together" (1:18). (Let's talk. Let's chat. Let's hang out. Let's have a conversation. Just you and me. And we'll both leave the stronger for it.) That's not what this gentleman wanted. He wanted to tell us that his way of believing was right and ours was wrong.

Here are some thoughts on how we can improve our relationships with people who hold opinions different from our own.

Flexibility over Umbrage

"Be devoted to one another in love. Honor one another above yourselves" (Romans 12:10).

As Robert D. Raiford says, "We have become the United States of the Offended." Casting ourselves as victims of other people's words means we never have to step up to the plate. It means we deserve sympathy. We don't have to take responsibility.

Political correctness has made us afraid to speak out. For many people, there's something satisfying about being the victim. You get sympathy and condolences. And it's a great way to maintain control. Rather than address a situation, you point a finger and say, "You offended me." You can turn an entire room against the "offender."

We can be like coiled springs of "offended" and as soon as someone says something we don't care for, our "victim response" springs into action. (Remember Dennis from *Monty Python and the Holy Grail*? "Help! Help! I'm being repressed.")

What if we entered into the conversation as if we were wearing a giant sign around our necks that said, "I could be wrong," and the person we're speaking with had one that said, "I could be right." If we approach conversations from that perspective, we can open the doors of communication that say, "I'll listen." That's a great place to start.

In youth ministry, the flexible leader knows that complaints come with the territory. You know what you're getting into. I took a few years of self-defense classes with my daughter. (She was reaching dating age, and it was either get her into a self-defense class or buy a gun.) One of the first things they teach you in aikido is how to fall. Keep your body rigid, and you'll hurt yourself. Learn to roll, and you'll be back on your feet immediately.

Stepping Up vs. Stepping Aside

Some people believe that the actual power or authority a youth minister wields in the church rates below that of the custodian. In truth, the actual power structure of the church looks like this:

1. Senior pastor: Perceived to wield the most power, whether he actually does or not.

2. Church secretary: Recognize her power if you ever want to get your mail or see your reimbursement check.

3. Custodian: People treat the custodian like a piece of furniture and speak in front of him about all manner of church business. If you really want to know the scoop, ask the guy who empties the trash baskets.

4. Music director—or the person in charge of the group that's been at the church the longest, whether it's the drama group, the nursery school, or the Ladies' Quilting Circle.

5. The guy who came in off the street to ask directions.

6. You.

Too often we allow that perception to become reality. When someone harrumphs, "You can't hold the youth pancake breakfast on that Sunday—why, that's when we've had the spring choir cantata for years," our first instinct is to back down, step aside, and reschedule the pancake breakfast for a time when it won't be in anyone's way—including the people who might have actually attended.

What if we did something new? What if we didn't have the annual pancake breakfast that was originally created by our pre-decessor's predecessor? What if our fundraising came from the of-fering from a youth-led worship service? What if we sold "youth stock" to raise money for the mission trip? What if we actually asked the board to fund our missions? If someone wants to be the heart and hands of Christ, should we really make him hold a bake sale first?

Resolving the "victim" conflict requires more than being as-sertive and shaking up old routines. It also involves refining your work relationships. For example, what if you established a policy making the youth group responsible for cleaning up after itself? What if the youth room were entirely the responsibility of the youth? If your group took one item off the custodian's to-do list, how much would you enhance your credibility with him? Or what if you showed up to a board meeting with typed notes and distributed copies to everyone? Part of resolving the "victim" con-flict is learning not to be the victim.

Important Instead of Urgent

"Whoever of you loves life
and desires to see many good days,
keep your tongue from evil
and your lips from telling lies.
Turn from evil and do good;
seek peace and pursue it." (Psalm 34:12-14)

When you get on a plane and begin that long taxi down the runway (the jaunt that makes you think you might actually be *driving* to your destination), your first order of business is to sit through the flight attendant's preflight instructions.

During the performance piece, most people read the in-flight magazine, the *USA Today* they found in the gate area, or the new paperback they bought in the terminal. Some fiddle with their luggage, their children, or their children's luggage. Only flight attendants, teachers, and pastors who have jobs that involve speaking important information to a crowd of people act as if they're listening.

What the flight attendant has to say is extremely important information. It's information that will save your life "in the event of an actual emergency." Yet most of us choose to focus our attention elsewhere.

The information is only important to us on one occasion: When the plane is actually going down. Then it becomes urgent.

If we're going to get along with people who think differently from the way we do, we must learn to tell the difference between what's important and what's urgent. Not liking the design of the new bulletin cover may be important to some people, but it's not urgent. Not being able to get enough volunteers for the church nursery and having to turn away young couples with small children as a result is important *and* urgent.

Knowing the difference between the two requires that both parties in question recognize the importance of an issue and then set priorities from there. In the case of differing theologies, it's important to recognize that we all serve a loving God. We all want to please him. And we all agree that the Bible is the most important book ever written.

Find common ground on the issues that are important to the continued growth of your church and then discuss from there. You'll find that many people are much more willing to talk rationally if they believe the things that are important to them have been acknowledged from the beginning.

Dishes

"Accept one another, then, just as Christ accepted you, in order to bring praise to God" (Romans 15:7).

There's an old adage that goes, "You can say things while you're doing the dishes that you can't say at the dinner table." When it comes to dropping a verbal bomb on your family, there are some things you can't say at the dinner table.

Susan: I'm quitting school.
Alison: I lost my job yesterday.
Bob: I'm dating a doctor. His name is Paul.

Such information is too blunt to be shared at the dinner table. After dinner, with your hands in the dish soap, is when you can approach these subjects more responsibly.

Maybe your church is having a problem of escalating tensions between the traditional and contemporary services. You can feel the "Us" and "Them" camps starting to develop. Sounds like a great opportunity for a community Easter egg hunt. Plan the activity, then invite members from all congregations to a daylong event where they can sit around the table and color eggs (or stuff candy into plastic ones, if you're concerned about such things as botulism).

If the Whispering Pines United Church of Christ sits across the street from the Cornerstone Evangelical Episcopal Church, maybe a joint MDA carnival or community concert is in order.

'Cause Me and God, We're Very Close

I was once in a meeting with my "youth council," a group of adults who oversaw the activities of the youth group. We were having a disagreement about how students who couldn't afford to attend an event could come up with the cash. My idea was to give it to them. The council's idea was to have them work the money off by "renting" themselves out to members of the congregation who needed to have their lawns mowed, pools cleaned, or dogs washed.

A woman who had three children in the group (which meant she would be on the youth council for the next eight years) said, "Steve, I prayed about this last night and I asked God to show me if my opinion was wrong, and since I didn't get any sort of sign, I'm pretty sure God agrees with me on this one."

I know, you're thinking how lucky I was to have someone on my youth board who was so close to God that she and he agreed with each other on most issues. How convenient, right?

Some people actually believe that what they decide is what God wants. That notion may come from holding an opinion for so long that it becomes like Scripture to them. The pancake breakfast is held on Easter Sunday between sunrise and the first service. Period. That fact is as real as Communion to some people. To mess with it would be like taking the wine out of Christ's hand and replacing it with a shoe, as far as they're concerned.

Can you respond by digging in your heels and saying, "I'm in charge, and we're going to do it *this* way"? Yes, you can, but you must ask yourself what you're willing to give up. Your collection of adult volunteers? Your budget? Your job?

Can you say, "Well, let's try it a new way for just this year and see how it works out"? Yes, you can, but then you must ask yourself, "How many of these people are going to put their best effort into making this a success if they know they only have to go along for one year?"

Here are the questions to consider before making a decision:
- How important is it to the overall program to have the pancake breakfast on Easter morning?
- How many parents (other than those in charge) would prefer to sleep in and spend the time together as a family?
- How important is it to the parents (those in charge) that their students actually worship together as a family on the day we celebrate the risen Christ?

Mustache Twirling
Some theologies don't work without a villain. In order for some

people to be right, someone else must be wrong. In order for *me* to stand up in my righteousness, *you* have to sit there in your wrongness. Some people simply must have a bad guy in order for their own personal theology to make sense. For them, heaven and the kingdom of God are things to be won, to be earned, to be fought for. And they are more than willing to fight.

You will rarely win an argument with someone who thinks like this. To suggest to them that they might be wrong simply feeds their belief that you're the embodiment of evil and must be destroyed. Likewise, you can't win an argument with an atheist. The one thing you cannot offer regarding the existence of God is proof. As Christians, our belief system requires faith. Faith cannot be held, smelled, heard, tasted, or seen. Therefore, you will not win the proof argument. The upside is that God has an influence over all lives—even those people who choose not to believe.

A Change Will Do You Good?

If you think making a change is your best option, MAKE THE CHANGE. Don't back down. Get some parental and staff support behind you before you take the plunge. Inform your boss of the potential storm that's headed her way. Provide alternatives for those who choose not to go along with the change. And make sure you're prepared to deal with the resulting loss and fallout.

Read Romans 14:5-6.

Yes, opinions differ, but ask yourself if you're using yours to build others up or to tear them down.

Three questions can be heard in any Christian church around the world:

- Do you believe in God? (I believe in God.)
- Do you believe in Jesus Christ? (I believe in Jesus Christ.)
- Do you believe in the Holy Spirit? (I believe in the Holy Spirit.)

This is where it all starts. This is where it all ends.

Memorize This

Treat change like an iceberg. Move slowly, but
let nothing stand in your way.

8. Carry My Rat

What? There's Stress in Your Job?

I love movies. I see all kinds of films just for the fun of going to the movies. It's a blast to me to sit in a crowd and watch a film. Some movies are better than others. Some suck me right into the story. Others leave me wanting to bang my head against a wall. You can be part of the story or you can be part of the crowd. Either way is cool. Most of the time an afternoon at the theater is time well spent. I see a lot of movies. I mean A LOT.

As far as I'm concerned, one of the most disturbing images in recent film history is from the 2003 movie *Willard*. This update of a '70's horror classic deals with a young man named Willard who learns to communicate with—and control—rats. There's a scene about midway through the film in which a set of elevator doors opens and a flood (I mean a FLOOD) of rats comes pouring out. As the elevator empties, we see Willard inside, standing among the rats. He'd packed himself into the elevator with thousands and thousands of the nasty little vermin (shudder). I don't like rats.

Okay, ready to talk about stress?

Stress? What stress? others may wonder. *Youth workers only work, what—one or two days a week? What stress can you possibly have in a church? It's not like it's a real job.*

Be that as it may, let's imagine for a moment that each item on your to-do list—each problem that causes you stress—is a rat. Not necessarily one of those big, slimy, stinky New York sewer rats that climb up plumbing pipes and bite you as you... well, you get the picture. Imagine they're mostly clean (but still quite ooky) lab rats.

These are your to-do rats. You might have three or four of them crawling around your desk right now. They're just sniffing around, not bothering anybody. Then you notice there are three or four on the floor. You've got several in your car. You're going to be packing up to leave soon, so you begin stuffing them into your briefcase or the messenger bag you got at the last YS convention. You shove a few rats in your pocket. You also let one or two ride on your shoulder.

You're on your way to a staff meeting. The rest of the people at the meeting have their own bag-o-rats, and their primary goal is to give as many of them to you as they can. The winner is the one who can leave the room with the least amount of rats.

Kind of puts a whole new visual on stress, doesn't it?

Too often when we think of stress, or when we say, "I'm really stressed out," the first thing we do is point the finger at someone else and say, "*That person* is the reason I'm stressed out." The stress is because of:

- That kid who never stops talking in meetings and makes the girls uncomfortable.
- My boss who, once a week, calls me into his office to tell me where I'm failing.
- My spouse, who doesn't get that I work on Sundays, and that lock-ins, retreats, and mission trips are part of the job.

We need to recognize that the stress we feel isn't always "inflicted" upon us. Often we CHOOSE to take it. We CHOOSE to accept somebody else's rat.

It doesn't have to be that way. You don't have to take somebody else's rat. You have enough of your own. If someone asks, try one of these replies:
- "My schedule is really full right now."
- "I'm up to my ears as it is."
- "You're so creative. I'm sure you can find a way to do it."

Why Didn't You Just Leave Me to DIE?

Take a look in Exodus sometime and you'll see the classic example of a dysfunctional congregation. Imagine a church congregation in Smalltown, Ohio, breaking free from the rule of a wildly abusive senior pastor. The church forms a search committee and hires a new pastor, who announces, "I'll lead you out of your situation, but it's going to be tough."

Congregation: "We don't care. Anything is better than this. We'll follow you!"

Six months later pledges are down, membership is down, and morale is down.

Congregation: "Oh, why didn't you just leave us alone? Why have you brought this misery on us?"

Moses dealt with that kind of complaining all the time. When the Israelites said they were thirsty, Moses went to God and he gave them rain. When they said they were hungry, God gave them manna. In response, they said they didn't like manna.

And what does Moses hear from the people? "You should have just let us die. We were slaves, but at least we had food. Why did you do this to us?"

Read Psalm 46 or 62. Or go crazy and read both of them.

Step back. Take a deep breath. Go outside for a moment. The Psalm writer puts his trust in God and is overwhelmed with a sense of calm. He sees his detractors as dust on his shirt. He realizes they have no real power in the long run.

It's all about taking a deep breath and saying, "Okay, God— *your* timing, not mine. I will be patient. I will wait on the Lord." Much of our stress comes from spending too much time trying to please our critics and not enough time trying to please God.

Melt Me, Mold Me, Punch Me, Squeeze Me

Picture a potter shaping a lump of clay. With the spinning wheel before him, the potter, using great care and skill, places his hands on the clay and forms it into a beautiful coffee cup. The cup is given time to dry and then placed in a kiln (furnace) and fired. After being given sufficient time to cool, it now sits on your desk holding your morning caffeine.

Those of you who know something about pottery know there's a step that comes before the shaping process. To prepare the clay to be molded, the potter slams it repeatedly against the wheel. Over and over the clay is pushed, pulled, rolled, and mashed. Sometimes it's cut in half with a small wire. The halves are then slammed back together and the process continues. (Does that sound like a staff meeting at your church?)

Why does a potter work the clay over in such a manner? And why does the Bible use that image to portray God's relationship with us?

The potter is trying to get the air bubbles out of the clay. Little pockets of air can keep the clay from sticking together. If a piece of pottery containing air pockets goes into a fire, it will explode.

When I was in high school I spent a lot of time in Mr. Dunn's art room. One year we spent several weeks working on clay projects, learning potting techniques and operating skills for the potter's wheel. Mr. Dunn had a kiln in his classroom. When our projects were dry, they were placed in the kiln and fired for several days.

One day when we were sitting in the classroom, we heard a loud "bang." Everybody jumped. Mr. Dunn explained that somebody's project must have had an air bubble in it. The explosion took out almost every other project in the kiln.

The slamming, the folding, the smashing are all methods of preparing you for the fire. God knows what's coming, and if you're not prepared you will not survive.

- "I didn't get the budget increase." (Slam.)
- "Jenny's parents are divorcing." (Slam.)
- "The youth group set off the fire alarm again." (Slam.)
- "The choir director scheduled the cantata for the Sunday after the lock-in." (Slam.)

Read Romans 5:3-4:

We also glory in our sufferings, because we know that suffering produces perseverance; perseverance, character; and character, hope.

When you're stressing out, take a step back and ask yourself, "What am I supposed to learn from this? What's being planted now to help me deal with something else later?"

I've been in youth ministry nearly 20 years now. I went from a place that didn't respect their youth ministers to a place that welcomed them. At the previous church, I was youth director number five in about seven years. Soon after I started, a "group of concerned parents" began meeting to discuss the problems in the youth group. (They didn't invite the youth director.)

My email began to fill with complaints and well-intentioned "just letting you know" letters. One woman tried to create her own group in her own house for her own child and the rest of his disenchanted friends.

That's why virtually no complaint can get under my skin these days. I went through 17 months of hell at my former church. What can mere mortals do to me now?

You have to go through the fire in order to get better at what you do. Your vase will not hold flowers—your cup will not hold coffee—if it has not been properly fired and allowed to cool.

Handcuffing Ourselves to Our Ministry

Did you know that the book of Philippians contains the word *joy* more than any other book in the Bible? Philippians 4:4-9 is a prime example. Yet Paul most likely wrote the book while he was chained to a wall. Think about that. You think *you* feel tied to your job? Paul was in actual chains, yet he managed to write about finding the joy that's within us.

The lesson is obvious. The stress we experience on the outside doesn't necessarily have to affect what we feel on the inside. Paul was living under the threat of death, yet he wrote about feelin' groovy.

Joy comes from the inside. It comes from being at the right place at the right time and knowing it. God placed you where you are. Even when you're having a bad day, there's still that tiny speck of joy that says, "I'm where God wants me to be." If joy is too hard at this point ... go for "satisfaction" and build on it.

You are a servant of God. No matter what happens, the Creator of the known universe (and the unknown universe beyond that) is right next to you, inside you and above you, beneath you and around you. God is here.

Take a deep breath. Go ahead. Right now. Put your finger in the book and take a deep breath.

God is still here.

Good Stress?

You can find thousands of books and articles out there on "Eliminating Stress" and "Making Stress a Thing of the Past." Manufacturers label products as being "stress free." Conventional wisdom suggests that people avoid stress whenever possible.

In some cases, though, stress may be a good thing. Stress can give you a goal. It can make you work hard and give you a challenge.

There was a woman who sat on my Christian Ed. committee. She was a nice, older lady who simply wouldn't try anything new. Every time I tried to come up with an idea that was new and creative, she'd say in a quiet voice, "Well, we've never— that is, I think we did that once before and it really didn't work out. But, oh, I guess if *you* think…I'm sure the kids won't be too disappointed."

Every meeting I knew she was going to be there and I knew she was going to go through the same routine. I just wanted to reach across the table and give her a dope slap (in Jesus' name, of course). One day we were planning the annual Christmas pageant. (Talk about your sacred cow.)

After I floated an idea, she started in on her response. I waited for her to say, "Well, I guess if *you* think so," then I interrupted and said, "Good, it's settled then." I went home and banged out the best Christmas pageant ever. *Everyone* was involved, from the oldest member of the congregation to the youngest. It was a thing of beauty. I don't think it would have ever happened if I hadn't so desperately wanted to show her that you could actually use a script that was written *after* 1964. That's what stress can do for you.

God Is in Group Work
Gather together a few youth workers in your area. Meet someplace away from the church for lunch—and for the chance to scream together in frustration. You don't have to solve each other's problems; you just have to listen to each other. You'll be surprised how much better you feel afterward.

Stress becomes bad when the goal we strive for is unobtainable. If your goals—whether you set them yourself or have them set for you—include doubling your group's membership, raising thousands of dollars, and getting your master's, you may be in for some stress.

Look at the big picture. Literally. Print out your entire calendar and tape it to the wall. See the whole year. See your whole budget. Count the number of Sundays you actually have to get something done. Fill in every meeting. Every fundraiser. Every event. Every game of your students that you attend. Set some priorities. Above all else, give yourself permission to say, "I'm doing enough."

Living Life at Full Speed

Read the following paraphrase of a passage from 2 Corinthians 11:18-33. Try reading it aloud as fast as you can. (Seriously.)

Oh, no, it's a bad habit I picked up from the three-ring preachers who are so popular these days. Since you sit there in the judgment seat observing all these shenanigans, you can afford to humor an occasional fool who happens along. You have such admirable tolerance for impostors, who rob you of your freedom, rip you off, steal you blind, put you down—even slap your face! I shouldn't admit it to you, but our stomachs aren't strong enough to tolerate that kind of stuff.

Since you admire the egomaniacs of the pulpit so much (remember, this is your old friend, the fool, talking), let me try my hand at it. Do they brag of being Hebrews, Israelites, and the pure race of Abraham? I'm their match. Are they servants of Christ? I can go them one better. (I can't believe I'm saying these things. It's crazy to talk this way! But I started, and I'm going to finish.)

I've worked much harder, been jailed more often, and was beaten up more times than I can count, and I've been at death's door time after time. I've been flogged five times with the Jews' 39 lashes, beaten by Roman rods three times, and pummeled with rocks. I've been shipwrecked three times and immersed in the open sea for a night and a day. In hard traveling year in and year out, I've had to ford rivers, fend off robbers, struggle with friends, struggle with foes. I've been at risk in the city, at risk in the country, endangered by desert sun and sea storm, and betrayed by those I thought were my brothers. I've known drudgery and hard labor, many a long and lonely night without sleep, and many a missed meal. I've been blasted by the cold and left naked in the weather.

And that's not the half of it, when you throw in the daily pressures and anxieties of all the churches. When someone gets to the end of his rope, I feel the desperation in my bones. When someone is duped into sin, an angry fire burns in my gut.

If I have to "brag" about myself, I'll brag about the humiliations that make me like Jesus. The eternal and blessed God and Father of our Master Jesus knows I'm not lying. Remember the time I was in Damascus and the governor of King Aretas posted guards at the city gates to arrest me? I crawled through a window in the wall, was let down in a basket, and had to run for my life.

Do those words have a familiar ring to them? Does it seem as though Paul is writing about your life? If so, it might be time to switch to decaf.

Somewhere among the full-speed-ahead, git-r-dun, I'll-sleep-when-I'm-dead moments is God. I picture him sitting in a lawn chair along some mystical beach. In his hand he has one of those drinks with a little umbrella in it. (Just picture it as pineapple juice if the idea upsets you.) He also has an empty chair beside him and he's wondering when you're going to stop running around long enough to stop and have a talk with him.

Mike Yaconelli wrote about seeing God in the "in-betweens" of life:

> Beginnings and endings. Starts and finishes. Those are the parts of life that grab my attention. God is found in the everydayness of life, in the middle of life. God is sneaking around in the ordinariness of each day, longing to be noticed, longing to be discovered. It is tragic that much of my life I have looked for God in the momentous, and instead He's been waiting in the moment. The passive life liberates us from a God of decisions to a God who is between decisions. No wonder my relationship with God is stunted! I have spent most of my life looking for God instead of being with God.

Pennies from Heaven

I'll wrap up this chapter with one more image from the New Testament. You'll find it in Romans 5:3-5 (*The Message*):

> There's more to come: We continue to shout our praise even when we're hemmed in with troubles, because we know how troubles can develop passionate patience in us, and how that patience in turn forges the tempered steel of virtue, keeping us alert for whatever God will do next. In alert expectancy such as this, we're never left feeling shortchanged. Quite the contrary—we can't round up enough containers to hold everything God generously pours into our lives through the Holy Spirit!

I love the image of God pouring blessings down and us standing outside with Tupperware containers to catch them. (I know it's weird, but that's how I see it.) People who live at full speed will run around, trying to catch individual raindrops. People who have learned to slow down, be still (Psalm 46), and live in the in-betweens will stand in the downpour and just hold out their containers.

Memorize This
The reason people bang their heads against a wall
is that it feels so good when they stop.

9. Stuff Happens

What to Do When the Worst Thing That Can Happen...Does

Let me tell you about Lewis.

Lewis was a big guy, stocky and strong. If you said, "Hey, Lewis, help me lift this Buick" and then walked around to help lift one end, he'd grab it in the middle, flip it up onto his shoulder, and grin at you.

Lewis had one of those incredibly gentle souls that often hide behind big exteriors. And he had one of those exteriors dogs and kids can see right through. Do you know what I mean? I took Lewis as part of a group to a shelter in Akron, Ohio. There were 10 teenagers in the room when a little guy, maybe four years old, poked his head around the corner. I had girl students who wanted to be teachers someday get down on their knees and say, "Come here. Can I see you?" They clapped their hands and opened their arms like they were inviting a hug.

The little guy walked right past them to big, gruff Lewis and held up his little arms. Lewis lifted him up and set him on his arm, and that kid didn't leave that spot for about five days. You can't be fake with little kids and dogs.

Lewis loved McDonald's. He had a gift for crap-detecting (especially mine). He liked his music loud and his cars fast. When Lewis graduated from high school, we sort of drifted apart. I had new students to tend to and he had a life to start. I saw him a few times after he graduated—once just to say "hi" and once when he told me he was engaged.

In November 2006, Lewis was riding his motorcycle (one of those small, fast ones) at night. He was traveling over a hundred miles an hour when a car pulled out in front of him. Lewis hit the side of an SUV and was killed instantly.

I got a call from Lewis' father to ask if I would do the funeral.

I'd spent my entire career with mostly happy, mostly upper-middle-class kids who got grounded, dated people their parents mostly approved of, went on mission trips, and only occasionally got into trouble at school. To be asked to preside over the funeral of a former student made me feel like I was one of those special-unit soldiers who gets dropped out of a plane with a spoon and a compass and told to find his own way home. I kept thinking, "I am so unqualified to do this."

The longer you do this sort of work, the better the chances are that you'll eventually have to bury one of your students—or teach a lesson about grace when madmen fly planes into buildings, or talk to a student when a classmate brings a gun to school, or counsel a student who confides in you that her father (uncle, teacher, boyfriend) did something unspeakable.

This is the hardest thing you'll do in youth ministry. Sometimes it burns and leaves a scar, but scars heal. If you're going to avoid burnout, you're going to have to learn to deal effectively with the worst-that-can-happen-just-did scenarios. This is the *ministry* part of youth ministry.

So what do you do? What is youth ministry when the bottom falls out of your—or someone else's—life?

Start Here: You Have No Idea What You're Doing

"Trust in the LORD with all your heart
and lean not on your own understanding;
in all your ways submit to him,
and he will make your paths straight" (Proverbs 3:5-6).

When I realized I had to visit Lewis' family, I asked my boss what to do. What's the process? I wanted to know. What methods do "real" ministers use when they have to visit a family to prepare for a funeral?

Here's what he told me: "Sit in your car outside the house and say, 'God, I have no idea what I'm doing. Please help me.' Then you go in."

Accept the fact that you're in over your head. Accept the fact that each moment is unique—one will not be like the next. There's no formula. There's no process.

Above all else, accept that as hard as this moment is for you, it's that much harder for the people who need you. This rule applies to every situation. If you have to sit down with a student while she tells you, "I think I'm pregnant" or "I'm gay" or "My dad hits me," that moment in time is nothing for you like it is for her.

Here are a few hints to help you get through the experience:

1. Do not panic.
"YOU'RE WHAT?!" is the exact wrong answer. If you're to the point where a young person is sitting with you, chances are either you or the young person initiated the sit-down; therefore, you should be prepared for anything. Overreacting will make your student overreact and may keep you from being able to help.

2. If the student is in danger of any kind, respond immediately.
Don't wait to talk about the situation in a few days. If the only thing you can do at that moment is call your boss, then do that. If there's danger, take action. Here in Florida it's called "mandated reporting." If a student tells a teacher about a dangerous situation, that teacher (or mentor or youth minister) is required by law to let the appropriate authorities know. Familiarize yourself with what your state requires and what's expected of you.

3. Even though you're the butt of many jokes, your students still see you as someone who has answers.
That's not to say you should act like you've got all the answers. I've found that when I try to pass myself off as Bible-Man in my meetings, some kid will come up with a whopper I have no clue about. You may not know all the answers, but you must listen to the entire question. Don't try to fix—just listen. Job's friends came to grieve with him and sat with him for *seven days* without ever saying a word. Then they opened their mouths and more

trouble started. When stuff happens, your first step should be to listen.

4. Don't cast the wide blanket of "Everything's Going to Be Okay" over everything.

Your students and their families listen to you. They trust you. If you say, "It's going to be all right," because that's what you think they need to hear...you've done them a disservice. If you're sitting in an emergency room because someone's dad had a massive coronary, "It's all going to be okay" is not the right answer. Let your students and their families know it's okay to be scared. It's okay to be angry. It's okay to be sad. That's assurance you can offer honestly.

5. If you're dealing with a massive tragedy, expand the invitation.

If you're facing a situation on the scale of 9/11 or Hurricane Katrina, encourage your students to invite their friends, neighbors, and acquaintances to your meeting. Dump the lesson plans and hold a prayer service. Consider other practical needs you can fill, as well. How quickly can you get food and blankets together? How quickly can you arrange for shelter? How quickly can you put a mission team together?

6. You can't force students to talk, unload, or spill their grief.

This can be a hard truth to accept, especially if you're convinced that talking is what your student needs to do. But trying to force your student to share with you is like picking at a water balloon with a pin. You keep poking little holes until it all comes spilling out. That's when you find you've made a mess and lost your balloon. Let the family or student know you're there to listen whenever they want to talk. If you haven't done so already, give kids your home number or cell number and tell them you'll listen whenever they want to talk. That way, when THEY are ready, you'll be the one they go to.

The Statue Cycle

There's a cycle that occurs frequently in the face of tragedy. Adults say to themselves, "We must be strong for the children." Tragic situations bring out the protective instinct in grown-ups—and anyone under the age of 20 becomes "the children." So for the sake of the children, adults keep their emotions in check and put up a brave front.

Teens then look to adults for clues as to how they should react. They see the adults being "strong" and then try to emulate them by being strong themselves. That causes the adults to start asking, "Why isn't Jimmy crying?" or "Why isn't Lisa showing her grief?" And the cycle continues.

Remember—it's okay to cry. It's okay to admit you're afraid. And it's okay to admit that don't have the answers.

Invite God

You'd be surprised how many ministers forget to include God in the process. We believe that God sent us to minister to the hurting. And when we're in full "minister mode," we tend to look to the heavens and say, "'Sokay, Big Guy, I got this one."

But if you remember to include God from the start, you'll find he opens his Word and uses Scripture to speak to us.

As I prepared for Lewis' funeral, his family told me stories about his love for fishing. I checked the Scriptures for fishing stories and came across passages involving Peter. Peter was the impetuous disciple. Always the first one in line. He was the one who stepped out of the boat to walk with Jesus on the Sea of Galilee. Yeah, he sunk like a rock (pun intended), and you know his buddies gave him a hard time when Jesus put him back in the boat. To which Peter might have replied, "Three steps! Did you see that? Let me see *you* do three steps."

Peter was the one who, later, according to Scripture, stood up in the boat, put his clothes on, and jumped in the water. (I'll repeat that for those of you who were skimming.) Peter put his clothes ON and then jumped in.

These two images were classic "Lewis behavior." I was able to use them in the funeral service. I was able to use the image of Jesus on the water saying, "Come." Jesus wrapped his arms around Peter and held him tight until he got his footing. I'm sure the same thing happened when Lewis' motorcycle hit the SUV. I believe Lewis flew directly into the loving and accepting arms of Christ.

Don't exclude God when you work with the people who most need to feel his presence. A group prayer to our heavenly Father is a powerful thing. Injecting the Holy Spirit into the room can do wonders.

Life Is Over

Teenagers can be remarkably shortsighted. To their credit, they can teach adults something about the beauty of living in the present moment. However, that focus on the immediate can work to a teenager's detriment in times of upheaval. Events we consider to be "nothing much" may seem like "the end of the world" to a teenager. An F on a midterm, a cheating boyfriend, or a crack from mom about weight can seem as tragic to a teenager as any tsunami.

Take a step back and think about your teenage years. We were hypersensitive to everything. A small remark became a knife in the back; a smile from a pretty girl became "Yeah, she's into me." Remember those times? Think about them before you start talking with a teen who's having a crisis-of-the-moment.

Talk with your teens about their childhood. Get them to tell you a story about when they were small. Get some perspective going. If you're dealing with a senior high student, ask something like, "Are you the same person now that you were when you were in junior high?" (The answer is no, but it may come in the form of a "duh" look.)

Say, "You've changed a lot, haven't you? I'm telling you you'll change that much again from this moment to when you're in college. And when you graduate college, you'll make an even bigger leap."

Don't dismiss their feelings. Don't try to say something like, "It's not as bad as you think" or "You'll get over it." Those are future comments. Teens are living now and as far as they can see, they *won't* get over it.

Try this: "Tomorrow will suck less." Get their attention. Then say, "The day after that will suck a little less than tomorrow. You just have to keep going until it doesn't suck at all."

I've used that last one several times and it's worked more than any other advice I've ever given.

God Is Not to Blame; God IS in Charge

Many Christians have a tendency to approach their faith as though God made the rose and the devil made the thorn. If we get a new baby in the family, we praise God. If Grandpa dies, we curse God. If someone is beaten or murdered or killed in an accident, we assume it's Satan's doing.

The fact is, God made the rose *and* the thorn. The thorn helps protect the rose. That's called nature, not Satan.

God doesn't punish people by taking away their grandmothers. He didn't send hurricanes to Central Florida because Disney offered benefits to same-sex couples.

"And we know that in all things God works for the good of those who love him, who have been called according to his purpose" (Romans 8:28).

This is a great verse to use when bad stuff happens. We can't blame God for what happens in our lives. God makes all things work together. He doesn't make bad stuff happen, but he takes *all things*—good and bad—and makes them work together. Our tragedies and our triumphs are of our own creation. God takes them and makes them work together.

And that leads us right into verse 29:

"For those God foreknew he also predestined to be conformed to the image of his Son, that he might be the firstborn among many brothers and sisters."

God predestined us to be like him—to have our lives reflect his. We know how the story ends. When we reach the end of our lives, be it by accident or by age, we wind up in the presence of God.

Just Let Me Feel Bad, Would You?

Let's say you're planning a quiet evening at home with someone special, by a roaring fire, with snow falling in big flakes outside. For mood music, are you going to put on the latest hardcore CD from the Slut Puppies?

No, you'll find the perfect tune to go with the mood. Likewise, if you're angry, you might put on some hard rock. If you just broke up with your boyfriend, you might play "K-tel's Greatest Breakup Songs."

Why, then, when someone dies or when tragedy shoves its way into our lives, do we think we have to compensate by looking up comforting Scripture passages?

A few years ago I heard a wonderful interview with Bono, lead singer for the group U2. He talked about looking at the Psalms in a new way. He referred to King David as Elvis. He explained that we need to learn to read the Psalms as if they were blues lyrics being sung by an old blind man in a smoky bar in New Orleans.

With the image of David as a blues singer in mind, I found a number of Psalms that got me through my rough patch. Here's one of them:

Psalm 22 (NIV)
For the director of music. To the tune of "The Doe of the Morning." A psalm of David.

My God, my God, why have you forsaken me?
Why are you so far from saving me,
so far from the words of my groaning?
O my God, I cry out by day, but you do not answer,
by night, and am not silent.
Yet you are enthroned as the Holy One;
you are the praise of Israel.
In you our fathers put their trust;
they trusted and you delivered them.
They cried to you and were saved;
in you they trusted and were not disappointed.

But I am a worm and not a man,
scorned by men and despised by the people.
All who see me mock me;
they hurl insults, shaking their heads:
"He trusts in the LORD;

let the LORD rescue him.
Let him deliver him,
since he delights in him."

Yet you brought me out of the womb;
you made me trust in you
even at my mother's breast.
From birth I was cast upon you;
from my mother's womb you have been my God.
Do not be far from me,
for trouble is near
and there is no one to help.

Many bulls surround me;
strong bulls of Bashan encircle me.
Roaring lions tearing their prey
open their mouths wide against me.
I am poured out like water,
and all my bones are out of joint.
My heart has turned to wax;
it has melted away within me.
My strength is dried up like a potsherd,
and my tongue sticks to the roof of my mouth;
you lay me in the dust of death.
Dogs have surrounded me;
a band of evil men has encircled me,
they have pierced my hands and my feet.
I can count all my bones;
people stare and gloat over me.
They divide my garments among them
and cast lots for my clothing.

There's nothing wrong with sharing some of David's blues lyrics with people who are hurting. "Let me feel like crap, just for now—just for the moment let me have my grief" is a perfectly natural request. And the Psalms are full of "I'm hurting" verses to help us accommodate that request.

Psalm 46 offers a great visual for the anger, pain, and frustration you feel after getting fired. It's one of those had-it-up-to-here snapshots. A giant "What do you want from me?!"

And God's voice comes in like a breeze and says, "Hush, I'm here. I'll always be here. I've got this under control."

Give yourself permission to feel like you're at the bottom of a deep well. It feels good for a little while, and then it gets a little boring. That's when it's time to climb out of the hole and move on.

Eventually you get over the breakup and listen to normal music again. Scripture speaks to us no matter where we are in our lives. Sometimes our job as ministers is to shut up and let it.

You Are Not Alone

If you look at the so-called comfort verses of the Bible, you'll find that one theme comes up again and again. (It's pretty much the running theme of the whole book.)

You are not alone.

Read any of the following passages:

- Exodus 4:10-12
- Ecclesiastes 4:10-12

- Matthew 11:28
- Matthew 14:13-14
- John 10:27-30
- John 16:33
- 2 Corinthians 4:16-18
- 1 John 3:2

You are not alone. You never were. You never will be. If there's only one message you take to those who need to hear something—anything—let it be this.

You are not alone.

Memorize This
Maybe God's not giving me the words at this moment so that I'll shut up and listen.

10. Myth-Understanding

Some Lies and Truths about Youth Ministry

There are some basic truths we have to understand if we're going to be effective youth ministers. Part of the reason that burnout occurs is that we spend so much time trying to change things that can't be changed.

We all know the classic prayer in which we ask for help to accept the things we can't change. Yet often when we're faced with such things, we run full force into a wall again and again thinking that maybe this time we'll get through—and leave a youth-minister-sized hole in the bricks, just like in cartoons.

Myths and Truths about Working with Youth

Being able to separate the myths from the facts in youth ministry will go a long way toward helping you avoid burnout. Here's a brief list of popular myths to get you started.

MYTH: Youth ministry is about numbers.

You're standing in the fellowship hall after the morning service. A church member with absolutely no animosity in his heart whatsoever—someone who simply wants to make conversation—approaches you. What's the first question that person's going to ask?

"How many kids do you have showing up on Sunday night?"

HOW MANY is the criteria by which the church board judges our success. Consequently, HOW MANY is the basis on which we tend to judge ourselves.

Have you ever noticed that the longer the previous youth minister is gone, the larger the number of students she had grows?

TRUTH: Youth ministry occurs in small, quiet, one-on-one settings.
Youth ministry occurs when you're sitting in the back of an auditorium on a Thursday night watching the world's worst production of *The Music Man* because one of your students has a solo. And you can't even sneak out during the intermission because she's going to look for you during the curtain call.

Youth ministry occurs during a lock-in when everybody else is watching the movie in the youth room and you're cleaning up pizza boxes and one kid offers to help and then says, "Can I talk to you about something?"

For those who need a goal, try to shoot for 10 percent. If there are 100 people in the congregation on a Sunday morning, then having ten kids in the youth group is just fine. If you already have more than that, you're golden. If you consistently have fewer than ten percent, you might want to work on your advertising.

MYTH: Youth ministry is about office hours.

There will always be churches that put a high priority on you being in your office when you're supposed to be, getting your newsletter articles in on time, and keeping track of the action plan for your five-year goals on a daily basis.

I once tried to explain to my boss that the reason I didn't spend more time in my office was that there were no teenagers there. (They didn't want to show up any more than I did.) He believed that if I kept consistent office hours, teens would come to see me.

TRUTH: You have to go where the teenagers are.

You have to be in the stands at the game, in the audience during the play, and alongside the road as the parade passes by. You have to find out if the local high school has a guest lunch program or an open lunch.

Youth ministry occurs *after* the Bible study meeting when five guys remind you that McDonald's has 99-cent Happy Meals after 8:00 on Wednesdays. So you shell out twenty bucks of your own cash and sit there eating large amounts of junk food with guys who just want to talk about cars and girls and school and girls and college and college girls and video games and...you get the idea.

The most effective youth ministry you do in your career will rarely take place within the walls of the church.

MYTH: "You can fix my kid."

Some parents bring their darlings to youth group with the hope that you will "fix" them. What the parents are really hoping is that you'll make their kids like them. Maybe junior has had a run-in with the law and, as part of his "punishment," he has to go to church. Or maybe the teen has started being disrespectful, defiant, and dopey. Whatever the case, the parents bring him to *you* to fix the problem. After all, isn't that what you get paid to do?

TRUTH: You can't fix a kid.

All you can do is open doors and illuminate possibilities. When it comes right down to it, you can encourage a young person to be herself, and that's about it. She has to make the decision. You can't push the kid out of the boat, but you can encourage her when she has to make the decision to step out into the storm. However, the ultimate decision as to who she is and who she's going to be is entirely up to her. And it's not your fault if she chooses to be a jerk.

MYTH: Students are servants of the church.

Isn't it amazing how concerned committees become about youth service projects when they need someone to wash dishes at the Spaghetti Supper? They might offer to feed your group or make a donation, but the invitation is less about eating the dinner and more about cleaning up after it. Committees that wouldn't even think of inviting the Ladies Quilting Circle to wash dishes have no problem inviting the youth to do it. Many of them even get offended when you decline the invitation.

TRUTH: Students are servants of God.

Someday we'll stop treating teenagers like they're "Christians in training." Service projects are a vital part of any youth program, but that doesn't mean you have to become indentured servants to the committees who plan the social calendar.

MYTH: Youth ministry is about helping youth become nice people.

The same people who complain that they never see the youth in the church service are the ones who complain when the youth slouch, pass notes, giggle, don't dress nicely enough, and eat all the "good" cookies after the service.

TRUTH: "Youth ministry" comes from the Greek translation for "messy noise."

(Don't bother looking that phrase up; it's a joke.) Church involves more than an hour on Sunday morning. Many youth show up for choir, youth meetings, Sunday school, *and* regular church services every week. It's not about getting polished up and sitting pretty on display. It's about making the youth presence known ("Look! We have teenagers in the building!") Invite the youth to church and have them sit behind your biggest detractor. When it comes time for the doxology, have them sing at the top of their lungs. Make your presence known.

MYTH: Youth should be present for all youth activities.

This is a hard one sometimes. There will always be kids who don't show up to the fundraiser and then still come for the pizza party. I admit there's a little part of me down deep inside that says, "That's not fair."

Then I think about the guy who sent workers out into the field at the end of the day and paid them the same thing he paid those who had been working since sunup. The vineyard owner—essentially, God—said, "What's it to you? It's my money and I'll do what I want with it." Who are we to argue with such reasoning?

TRUTH: There's no such thing as an inactive member.
I have a student, and I'm guessing you have one similar to him. He's a good kid. Parents are divorced. Mom makes him show up. Dad does not. He plays baseball. He has a girlfriend. He has a part-time job and maintains a solid A average in school. I'm lucky if I see him once every other month. When we have students like that, we should be dancing on the tables when they walk through the door. "Whooooooo-hoooooooooo! You're here!"

You can't say to a kid like that, "I'm sorry, but you didn't attend four meetings and one fundraiser so you aren't eligible for the mission trip discount."

MYTH: Youth ministry is about giving kids the answers.
This is a myth that's tempting to fall for. Passing yourself off as the one with the answers is a great way to earn "cool points" from your students—especially if you've been at this a long time. Teenagers have a need to see the world in black and white. That's part of what makes them susceptible to cults and groups that say, "We'll give you all the answers."

TRUTH: Anyone who says he has all the answers is either lying or selling something.
You *don't* have all the answers. The good news is, you can gain respect from your students when you say, "I don't know what I think about that either, so let's work it out together."

Our job as ministers is to protect the questions. Let there be a mystery to faith. Let there be a sense of wonder and searching. You should be asking *more* questions, and not just answering the ones in front of you.

Belief is nothing if you don't know what you believe in. We have to teach kids that faith is stepping out of the boat whether you have all the answers or not. Even the disciples didn't get it all the time. Jesus was constantly saying something to the effect of, "You still don't get it, do you?"

Matthew 28:17 tells us that even at Christ's resurrection "they worshiped him; but some doubted." You can have questions and still be Christian. If complete and total faith were the requirement for church membership, there would be no churches.

Encourage questions—then ask some more.

MYTH: Mission trips are about serving others.
True enough—but service isn't the *only* purpose for mission trips. Some of your teens may be after the community service points. Others enjoy the feeling they get when they give themselves away. But a mission trip is more than that.

TRUTH: Mission trips are about turning teens into disciples.
They're about those quiet worship services you have at night. They're about taking teens out of their comfort zones and saying, "This is what *agape* looks like."

Finally...

MYTH: Youth ministry is a "stepping-stone" to "real" ministry.
I remember finishing a youth Sunday when we had 20 teenagers leading the worship service, writing prayers, preaching, singing, and reading. All the kids used their own gifts for the service. I had my artists create the bulletin covers and my tech guys create

a PowerPoint presentation. It was perfect. I was really feeling great about myself. Then someone came up after the service and said, "That was so nice. So, when are you going to be a 'real minister'?"

TRUTH: There is no higher calling than ministering to youth. The truth is that if you're working with teenagers as a paid professional or as a volunteer driver for youth events or anywhere in between, you are a real minister in every sense of the word.

I'm not telling you anything you don't already know, am I? Many churches don't get it when it comes to youth ministry. Staying in the game requires commitment and an ability to let things roll off your back. People's comments and attitudes can feel like darts. Just a little stab of pain is no biggie, but after a while the pain can build up and make you want to bail out.

This is where God called you. If your church can't see that what you do is "real" ministry, you either have to keep doing what you're doing and find satisfaction in God's approval and not your church's, or begin looking for a church who sees your ministry as ministry.

And that takes us into the last chapter. Ready to learn a new word?

Memorize This
"Speak, LORD, for your servant is listening" (1 Samuel 3:9).
(Say that every morning and then actually listen.)

11. It's Better to Burn Out Than to Fade Away[3]

The Art of Winnowing

Find the problem and fix it or become irrelevant? Hmmmmmmmm.

When I was in college, I worked as a "student employee" for the local National Public Radio station. I was a communication major, and the station offered several part-time gigs each semester. They were coveted "real world" jobs for those who wanted to go into broadcasting. (At the time I had no thought whatsoever about being a youth minister.)

Each year we would record the National Folk Festival. Bands and singers from all over the country would show up for a weekend of folk music performances. There were shape note singers, choirs, lots of mandolins, Woody Guthrie wannabes, German quartets, and New Orleans blues bands. One year the producers of the event decided they wanted to bring in a younger crowd, so they invited a team of break-dancers from New York. They justified the booking by billing it as Modern Folk Dance (which, in a way, it was). During the big evening concert, the radio producer and all the assistants usually sat in the recording truck. When the break-dancers took the stage, because of the visual nature of their

[3] From the song "My My, Hey Hey (Out of the Blue)" by Neil Young and Jeff Blackburn.

act, the station went to programmed music. We, the assistants, went out to the front of the stage to watch the performance.

The concert took place in northeast Ohio. If you've ever been to northeast Ohio, you know it's not uncommon to have a hot summer day turn into an incredibly cold night as the wind comes in off Lake Erie. That's what happened on the night of the concert. The dancers, under the hot stage lights, started to move. As they did, their bodies started to steam. You could see the vapors rising off the young men with every pop and spin they did. I'd never seen anything like it.

Let's (Re)Learn a New Word

I told you that story so I could tell you this one. There is a process referred to in the Bible called "winnowing." Winnowing works like this. Harvested grain is placed in a "winnowing circle," an area made specifically for the task. Men go out in the cool of the evening with their winnowing forks, which look like a cross between a pitchfork and a show shovel. They scoop a shovelful of grain and throw it into the wind, only to have the wind blow it back at them.

You can't do winnowing in the morning because the wind usually isn't strong enough. You can't do winnowing in the afternoon because there's no wind at all. Winnowing must be done in the evening, when the wind is hard enough to blow the seed back at you.

Scoop a shovelful of grain. Throw it. Get it blown back. Throw it. Get it thrown back. Throw it. Get it thrown back.

When the process is repeated over and over, the grain husks start to break away from the seed. (Think of the candy-coated shell breaking away from an M&M.) Another worker actually separates the husk from the seed, but the winnowing begins the process.

Here's where the first story comes in. I picture guys going out to do the winnowing at night. They take their lanterns. It's hot, but there's a cool breeze coming in. There had to be some sort of winnowing work song. I picture them singing as they worked, getting a rhythm going, their bodies starting to steam.

There are times when youth ministry feels a lot like winnowing. Youth ministers work the hours nobody else wants to work. We do the same thing over and over, throwing seeds into the air, only to have them blown back in our faces. Sometimes, if we try working at the wrong time, the seeds we throw just fall to the ground. There are songs we sing just to make the time go quicker.

Somebody else down the line gets to do the actual separation of the "husk" and the "seed." We're out there in the winnowing circle, shoveling and throwing, shoveling and throwing, hoping that whatever husk or shell is covering your students' true selves is going to break away. That's what drives us to keep shoveling and throwing, shoveling and throwing.

Under those conditions, it's very easy to feel burnt out.

The 18-Month Myth
People quote this figure like it's gospel. "Most youth workers last

only 18 months." If you look at the facts, however, you'll find that just isn't true. "I've been trying to track down and kill that one for years," says Rick Lawrence, editor of GROUP Magazine:

> I've attempted to trace this now-infamous truism back to a specific source, and I can't find one anywhere. Gallup doesn't cite a particular study. Neither does Barna. It's a ghost vampire not even Buffy can kill. The 18-Month Myth is now part of youth ministry lore. It's been used over and over to describe youth ministers as easily scared gypsies who bolt at the first sign of trouble.
>
> Well, I'm here to tell you it's all a bunch of bunk. For years I've challenged people who reel off this 18-month statistic to cite their sources. I've disputed its authenticity for two reasons: (1) The average GROUP reader has five years of paid youth ministry experience and has stayed at the same church—both as a volunteer and paid staffer—for more than six years. (2) At conventions, workshops, and in casual conversations with youth ministers all over the country, I hardly ever meet one who bags it after a year-and-a-half.
>
> So we here at GROUP decided to find out the truth, once and for all. We asked our research staff to complete a scientific survey of North American churches using a representative sampling of denominations. Here's what we discovered:
> - The average paid youth minister has just over four years' experience (4.2 years, to be exact).
> - The average paid youth minister has been at the

same church for almost four years (3.9 years, to be exact).

So you're not the lone stable person in a sea of here-today, gone-tomorrow gadabouts. And, if you're a GROUP subscriber, it's a good bet you're even more committed to your profession and your church than those nefarious nonsubscribers out there. Now I feel all squishy inside—the good kind of squishy. I hope you do, too. (Rick Lawrence, *100 Youth Ministry Gems*)

Signs of Genuine Burnout

Whether you've been in youth ministry for 18 months or 18 years, there are some issues to keep an eye out for that can have a serious effect on your future.

No Vision

Sitting down with your boss to plan out your five-year goals is not the same thing as having a vision for your youth ministry. The goal for youth ministry is pretty much the same year in and year out: "Get teens to meet Jesus." And I don't need an "action plan" or a "movement chart" to tell me how that's going.

However, every youth worker should be able to answer four simple questions about his ministry:
1. Who are we?
2. Where did we come from?
3. Where are we going?
4. What do we believe?

If each week of your ministry is pretty much the same…if the mission trip is becoming old hat and easy to do…if you haven't felt challenged by your students in a while, chances are you may be experiencing a lack of vision.

No Heart

I love my kids. I love my job. I love the people I work with. I love the people I work for. I'm supported and appreciated, but for some reason my heart is just not in my ministry anymore.

Losing heart can happen when—
- We see our numbers start to dwindle.
- We spend hours preparing a lesson, only to have one girl with some fresh gossip suddenly command the attention of everyone in the room.
- The board cuts the budget.
- We see the little kid who came into our junior high program graduate from high school.
- That one kid we really thought we'd connected with is busted for possession.

These circumstances—not to mention the hundred or so others you can name—can do more than just break your heart. They can steal your soul.

Everyone is entitled to an occasional case of the "Sleep-Deprived Nasties." That's the mental condition that occurs on the fourth day of a five-day mission trip when that little twerp with the milkshake is going to make that "snooooooook" sound when he gets to the bottom of the cup, even though he knows how much it annoys you. What's more, he's going to look you right in the eye when he does it.

Yeah, we all get those. But when that feeling starts to domi-nate—when things that would have bounced off you in the past now stick in your skin like pointed darts—you may find that you've lost your joy, your heart for ministry.

You've heard it said that joy is contagious. Well, so is discon-tent. And discontent spreads even faster than joy.

No Prize in the Cereal Box
Have you ever pulled through the drive-thru of a fast-food restau-rant, had the nice lady hand you your bag of munchies, and then discovered you're missing your french fries when you're halfway home? Have you ever bought cereal so you could get the glow-in-the-dark necklace advertised on the box, only to find that it's not inside?

Youth ministry can create similar disappointments. We put our lives into our job—our job being our kids' lives—only to watch the kids graduate and move away, never to be heard from again. We plant seeds and somebody else gets to sit in the shade. We prune off the bad branches and we never find out if the tree bore fruit. The longer you stay in youth ministry the more of a problem this becomes—not to mention a more likely cause of burnout.

The Sick Church Syndrome
Symptoms of dysfunction in a church are a lot like those in in-dividuals. Certain churches can be addictive, nasty, controlling,

feeble, bipolar, and victimizing. We've all heard about churches that eat youth workers alive. I was at one. It was led by some dysfunctional people who all brought their baggage to church with them. The church resembled the lost luggage section in an airport.

When a sick church begins to support dysfunctional behavior, workaholic tendencies, and codependency, we take our own problems and throw them into the cycle with everyone else's. Imagine throwing your own personal dysfunctions on a merry-go-round with everyone else's, then watching as the ride spins faster and faster until all those dysfunctions start shooting out the sides and colliding with anyone standing in the way.

The overall health of your church is a major factor in how long you stay in youth ministry. And as is the case with any addictive behavior of an individual, you're not going to fix it. You just get sucked into the vortex of the dysfunction. If longevity in youth ministry is your goal, you may have to decide carefully where you're going to fulfill that goal.

Fixing the Hole
There are some things you can do to help put your soul back on track and avoid burnout in ministry:

1. Monitor your own spirituality.
Before you assist students with their spiritual lives, you need to make sure yours is in good condition. Here are a few "musts" to keep in mind:

You must carve out your own prayer time.

In the middle of the chaos that is your life, you have to find time to be silent with God. At the end of a meeting, after everyone else has gone home, sit in the dark sanctuary and talk to God. He wants to know how you think things are going. He wants to help. He wants to send his Spirit. Private moments with God are essential to your spiritual health. But no one is going to hand these moments to you. You have to make them happen.

You must be part of church, not just a leader.

It's funny how people forget that ministry is your job. You do it for a living (at least, some of you do). People assume that because you're in church, you have the same opportunity to worship God that the rest of the congregation has. They don't understand that there's a huge difference between leading worship and being part of the congregation. Take the time to sit in the congregation during a worship service. (If you have a chance, see if you can do it in another church so you aren't thinking about what you should be doing or what others around you think you should be doing.) Corporate worship is important. You can't neglect it in favor of your job.

You must continue your education.

What if you were in a used bookstore and picked up a copy of *Tom Sawyer*? Would you read it and decide that you never had to read another book again as long as you live? Of course not. The world moves on. Times change. Culture and society change, and you have to keep up with them. Take a class. Find a wealthy member of the congregation to foot the bill for you to attend a convention. Make yourself better at what you do.

You must network.

Remember that whole "You are not alone" thing from chapter 9? Well, sometimes you have to make that happen. There are other youth ministers in other churches in other denominations who are going through the same thing you're going through. You're very close to the end of this book. When you finish, when you close that back cover, pick up a phone and call a nearby church. Find a youth worker you don't know and invite him to lunch. Just lunch—not a joint, out-of-the-country mission trip. A burger. Then see where it goes.

You must take time off.

Taking kids to the beach for a weekend shouldn't count as part of your vacation time, no matter what that person on the administrative board said. (If someone pulls that kind of stuff on you, invite him to be chaperone on the next retreat. He'll rethink that policy pretty quickly.) Mike Yaconelli was a big proponent of time off. He thought all youth ministers should get one day a week off to do nothing but recharge. He also believed youth ministers should get one week a month and one month a year to renew their souls with rest and relaxation. Needless to say, that isn't going to happen. But if you don't find the time to take off and spend it alone or with your long-suffering youth minister widow (widower), you'll find yourself burned out ahead of your time.

2. Remember that this is a calling.

If you are here, then God called you. In my opinion, there is no higher calling than youth ministry. People love to work with little kids. Little kids give hugs and act like they're genuinely happy to see you. People like to work with adults because adults can carry on adult conversations. People like to work with "building project" ministries because you can see what you've done. You can stand on it. You can put your hands on it. It's an accomplishment that's solid. It's "there." It's substantial.

But most people are scared to work with teenagers. If you're doing what other people are scared to do, it's because God has looked into all that you are and decided that you should be working with one of his most prized creations. That's not a joke. That's a compliment.

3. Understand that youth ministry does not involve a method or formula.

Youth ministry is an ongoing, never-ending, constantly changing course of action. One of the beauties of youth ministry is that it will never be an office job. There's some office work required, but it will never be an "office job." If you try to make it one, if you try to lead it the same way you've been leading it for years, you're setting yourself up for burnout.

4. Remind yourself what you are *not* in this business for.

You're not here to make money. There is none.

You're not here for fame and glory. They are fleeting at best.

You're not here to "fix" kids. You're here to make them better disciples. (That doesn't mean making them "perfect." It means helping them get closer to their Creator.)

You're not here as a stepping-stone to "real" ministry. Youth ministry *is* real ministry. When you're sleeping in a sleeping bag on a concrete floor after having just (semi) digested yet another cheeseburger after spending the entire day serving and cleaning at a homeless shelter 500 miles from your home and some kid in the dark says, "Why does God allow that to happen?" it doesn't get any more "real" than that.

Finally, Understand This...

The Creator of the universe (known and unknown), the Being who is love...who constructed angels...who put the stars in the sky...who inspired the creation of every single flavor of Ben & Jerry's—that Being, that Creator and creating God—asked YOU to be his servant.

That's why you do what you do.

And in case no one else has said it...thank you.

Memorize This
Whatever don't kill you makes you stronger.

In *Youth Ministry 3.0*, you'll explore, along with Mark Oestreicher and the voices of other youth workers, why we need change in youth ministry. You'll get a quick history of youth ministry over the last 50 years. And you'll help dream about what changes need to take place in order to create the next phase of youth ministry—the future that we need to create for effective ministry to students.

Youth Minsistry 3.0
A Manifesto of Where We've Been, Where We Are,
and Where We Need to Go
Mark Oestreicher
RETAIL $12.99
ISBN 978-0-310-66866-4

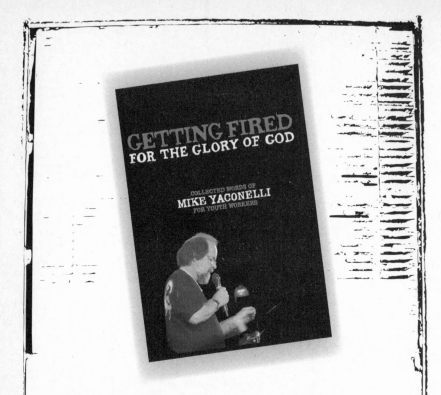

Years after his death, Christians across the world turn to the words of Mike Yaconelli to uncover the divine mischief, the shameless truth-telling, the love of kids, and the passion for Jesus that make youth ministry an irresistible calling. A DVD containing video and MP3 audio speeches is included.

Getting Fired for the Glory of God
Collected Words of Mike Yaconelli for Youth Workers
Mike Yaconelli
RETAIL $16.99
ISBN 978-0-310-28358-4

In this DVD series from the Skit Guys, you'll find six weeks of everything you need to teach a memorable lesson to your students on topics that really matter to them. Tommy and Eddie provide you with a Skit Guys video, a message outline, and small group questions for six different lessons on each DVD—making it easier than ever for you to plan a lesson!

You Teach Vol. 1
Videos, Study Guides, and Message Outlines
The Skit Guys
RETAIL $39.99
ISBN 978-0-310-28084-2

You Teach Vol. 2
Videos, Study Guides, and Message Outlines
The Skit Guys
RETAIL $39.99
ISBN 978-0-310-28085-9

You Teach Vol. 3
Videos, Study Guides, and Message Outlines
The Skit Guys
RETAIL $39.99
ISBN 978-0-310-28086-6

visit www.youthspecialties.com/store
or your local Christian bookstore

youth
specialties

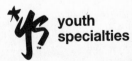

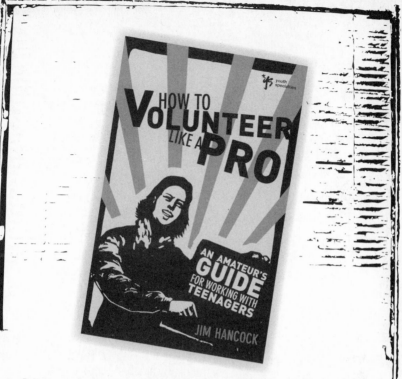

Being a volunteer youth worker can be exciting, intimidating, fulfilling, and challenging, and until now, there was no "manual" on how to be a volunteer in a youth ministry. *How to Volunteer Like a Pro* offers practical help and indispensable insights that will make your experience as a volunteer youth worker valuable and rewarding for you and your students.

How to Volunteer Like a Pro
An Amateur's Guide for Working with Teenagers
Jim Hancock
RETAIL $12.99
ISBN 978-0-310-28776-6

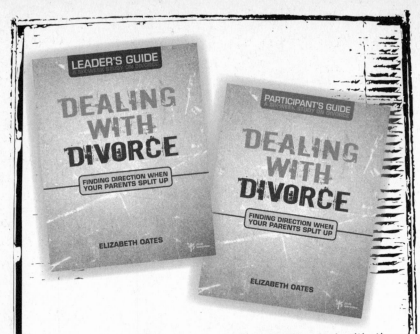
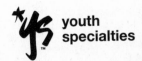